BRIAN H EDWARDS

God's little people:

Little women
in the Bible

DayOne

© Day One Publications 2006
First printed 2006

ISBN 1-84625-025-0

9 781846 250255 >

Unless otherwise stated, all Scripture quotations are from the
New International Version copyright © 1973, 1978, 1984

British Library Cataloguing in Publication Data available

Published by Day One Publications
Ryelands Road, Leominster, HR6 8NZ
☎ 01568 613 740 FAX 01568 611 473
email—sales@dayone.co.uk
web site—www.dayone.co.uk
North American—e-mail—sales@dayonebookstore.com
North American—web site—www.dayonebookstore.com

Designed by Steve Devane and printed by Gutenberg Press, Malta

Contents

What I love about the New Testament letters is that they are not just religious wise sayings. Most religious books in the world are just that—if wise they are. They are not rooted in history and they could have been written at any time by anyone. Therefore they cannot be checked for accuracy because there is no history about them.

The Bible is wholly different; in fact it is unique because it is constantly rooted in history all through the Old Testament and into the New Testament. So much of the Old Testament contains stories of actual people who, in their day, would have been quite insignificant: a childless wife, a godly woman in an unhappy marriage, a starving widow and her dying son, and a little servant girl in a foreign country. Similarly all the Gospels are about people who really lived and who met with Jesus; and the letters of Peter, Paul and the others, were dealing with real problems of real people in real situations; these people actually lived—and that makes them living letters.

If ever we find ourselves reading through Romans, for example, and concluding: 'I find Paul's letter to the Christians at Rome hard going', we should remember that some of those who read it first had not been converted more than a handful of years, and they were expected to understand the letter.

But there is another reason why I so love the letters of the New Testament. The lists of greetings by Paul make exciting reading. Take the list in Romans 16. With a few exceptions like Priscilla and Aquila, what Paul says about almost any person he names, contains all that we know. They appear so briefly and are gone. That is why we can all identify with them. They, like us, are God's little people. A few years after we have passed beyond this life, we will all be largely forgotten. Yet everyone of these little people achieved something for God. In Romans 16:13 Paul seems to have had a loss of memory that the Holy Spirit allowed to pass: 'Greet Rufus, chosen in the Lord, and his mother, who has been a mother to me too.' Paul appears unable to recall her name at the moment of writing, but what a great ministry she had to be like a mother to the apostle himself.

These are the days of awards: the Oscars and Emmies, the Brit Awards and Golden Globe, the Booker prize for literature, the Turner prize for art, and prizes for sport and music and just about everything else. To cap it all, the Queen herself rewards some of her citizens on her birthday and at the

New Year: everyone from sports personalities to politicians, and from lock-keepers to lollipop ladies. The winners are those who have achieved something noteworthy. They have served better, performed better, sung better, written better, painted better than others. But the greater number of her citizens live, work and pass out of this world without so much as a royal wave of the hand. And the greater tragedy is that many of them will have no reward beyond the grave to look forward to either. But in our lists there is a wholly different dimension.

None of God's little people expected to be sung heroes two or three millennia after their death, and there are hundreds more whom God could have chosen to set before us as examples; but they are here on the pages of Scripture to remind us all that the Sovereign of the universe uses little people to fulfill his great plan. In leading the church constantly forward 'in triumphal procession in Christ' (2 Corinthians 2:14), whether before the birth of the Messiah or after, it is spiritual lock-keepers and lollipop ladies that make up the bulk of his army. In God's plan, the last shall be first, the least are the greatest, and the servant is recognized and rewarded.

Everything in the Bible is significant. It is significant because all of it is God's word. He gave it, and he gave us all that he wanted us to know—no more and no less. Therefore what we read in the Bible must be significant because it comes from God. It is significant also because so much more could have been written. We have only one thousandth part of all that Jesus taught and did during his three years of public ministry. The apostle John tells us that there was so much more that if it was told there would not be enough books in the whole world to include it all (John 21:25).

In the Old Testament it is just the same. From the life of Moses to the end of Malachi we hurry through eleven hundred years; and although the Old Testament is a large part of the Bible, it contains a very small description of those years of important history. There is much more that could have been told.

So, every story and every person, however fleeting, must be important because 'everything that was written in the past was written to teach us, so that through endurance and the encouragement of the Scriptures we might have hope' (Romans 15:4). These short stories of a few of God's little women are told with that end in mind.

Hannah—a prayer of faith and a faithful prayer

'In bitterness of soul Hannah wept much and prayed to the Lord. And she made a vow, saying, "O Lord Almighty, if you will only look upon your servant's misery and remember me, and not forget your servant but give her a son, then I will give him to the Lord for all the days of his life"' 1 Samuel 1:10

We know more about Hannah and her relationship to her son than about any of the mothers in the Old Testament. That must make her significant, and if so, why did the Holy Spirit select so much about Hannah? Although she comes on the scene suddenly and within two chapters she has gone, those chapters are packed with information. No doubt one reason for her importance is that we cannot overestimate the significance of the influence of a mother upon her family.

Hannah's is a beautiful story and it is rich in instruction, because her influence upon Samuel was enormous, and that is why the Scriptures tell us what kind of woman she was. In case we are in danger of assuming that Hannah somehow came from a simple nomadic situation where life was plain and uncomplicated, we need to remember some of the difficulties confronting her faith.

Personal tragedy

Hannah was childless. There is agonizing stress, even today, for a woman who longs for a child but is unable to conceive—but it was even more so in Hannah's day. Although she could not have known Psalm 127:3, because it had not yet been written, it expresses the value of a male heir at that time: 'Sons are a heritage from the Lord, children a reward from him.' Not to have children in Bible times was seen as a blight from God. If children were a reward, the barren womb was a curse, and the implication was always that it was a punishment for disobedience.

There are at least two illustrations of this. To save his own life, Abraham had lied to Abimelech the King of Gerar by claiming that Sarah was only his sister. Abimelech took her into his harem but immediately God closed the wombs of all the women in his household as a judgement. When Abimelech realized this he at once handed Sarah back to her husband and 'Abraham prayed to God, and God healed Abimelech, his wife and his slave girls so they could have children again, for the Lord had closed up every womb in Abimelech's household because of Abraham's wife Sarah' (Genesis 20:17–18). Then again, as a reward to the Hebrew midwives in Egypt at the time of the slavery of the Jewish people under the pharaohs, God gave them families of their own (Exodus 1:21). As the barren womb was seen as a curse, so fruitfulness was seen as a blessing from God. The more children a woman had, the more God was pleased with her. There was, then, a social stigma about the woman who could not conceive. It was as bad as having a child outside marriage. When Rachel could not conceive, she cried out in desperation to Jacob 'Give me children, or I'll die!' (Genesis 30:1).

There are many women today who know something of the pain of this. They can enter into that deep personal tragedy of Hannah. However, she was deeply loved by her husband, and this is touchingly expressed by Elkanah: 'Hannah, why are you weeping? Why don't you eat? Why are you downhearted? Don't I mean more to you than ten sons?' (1 Samuel 1:8). This was so typical of the man who tries to bury his head from the problem and pretend that it was either not there or could easily be resolved. Elkanah failed to realize that Hannah's broken heart was a different kind of need. To be embraced by her husband and to embrace her own child were two very diverse emotions; the one does not easily and lightly take the place of the other.

Hannah was in a desperate turmoil in her whole heart and mind. She was in bitterness of soul (v 10), and that is a good translation because the word 'bitter' is a very strong word. Bitterly disappointed, she was finding it hard to accept God's will. That too is a not uncommon Christian experience when we find it hard to accept God's will or are resentfully disappointed in the way something has turned out.

Hannah betrayed the fact that she was in 'great anguish and grief' (v 16)—and she was not overstating her case. She attended an important religious festival (vs 8–9), but while everyone else was eating the good food, she could not enjoy it; she did not feel like eating. Elkanah asked her what was wrong, even though he should have known. Apparently she stayed for the meal—to be polite and pious, but as soon as the meal was over, she slipped into the Tabernacle to pray.

It was there that Hannah made her vow to God, though perhaps she had made it many times before:

O Lord Almighty, if you will only look upon your servant's misery and remember me, and not forget your servant but give her a son, then I will give him to the Lord for all the days of his life (v 11).

It was not difficult to make a promise like that. Under the pressure of her confused mind and yearning emotions Hannah would promise anything; she was desperate. Promises under pressure are easily made and quickly broken. However, this woman kept her promise to the very letter.

Domestic rivalry

In addition to her own personal tragedy was the abuse she received from Peninnah. Peninnah was the other woman in the home. Elkanah's unwise decision was to take a second wife and Peninnah bore him sons and daughters and the two women became rivals. There was no sympathy on the part of Peninnah; she had no concern and no heart that went out to the other woman in the home. Peninnah never once expressed her sorrow that Hannah could not have children; she never put a sympathetic arm around her shoulder or sat and wept with Hannah. On the contrary, she was the one who was producing the children and it was through her that the name of her husband Elkanah would be continued. She bore him sons—which were much more important than daughters—and she provoked Hannah to anger by constantly jibing her for her barren womb. We can imagine her parading her growing brood in front of this distraught woman. At every opportunity she would make it hard for Hannah. It went on day after day and year after year (v 7). A relentless, taunting mockery. Three is too many in any marriage.

At that time, what Elkanah had done in taking two wives was not against the moral law of God, but it was certainly contrary to God's natural law. God had allowed it at times in the Old Testament as a concession to sinful nature, just as he allowed divorce for the same reason, but it was very rarely a happy arrangement. It spoiled King David and dragged Solomon from his greatness.

By the time of the New Testament, the practice had been rejected by the Jews and this was reinforced by Jesus and the apostles. Jesus reminded the crowd: 'At the beginning the Creator "made them male and female"' and added, '"For this reason a man will leave his father and mother and be united to his wife, and the two will become one flesh." So they are no longer, two but one. Therefore what God has joined together, let man not separate"' (Matthew 19:4–6). The Creator's original perfect plan was one man and one woman—not one man and two women, and not one man with three women.

This pattern has normally been accepted by evangelicals without question, but in the eighteenth century an evangelical, Martin Madan, made the foolish suggestion that polygamy was to be recommended for social reasons. He pointed out, correctly, that men generally died younger than women and therefore Madan claimed that it would be very helpful if men could take more than one wife because it would go some way to alleviate the problem of destitute widows. He was rounded on by his fellow evangelicals, and our national poet, William Cowper, was one of those who turned on him. Cowper wrote a little ditty to show the folly of this:

If John marries Mary and Mary alone,
'tis a very good match between Mary and John.
Should John wed a score, oh the claws and the scratches
It can't be a match, 'tis a bundle of matches.

It was not one of Cowper's literary masterpieces but it made the point, and that is exactly what we find here in the home of Elkanah: claws and scratches. There was no love lost between these two women. Hannah could find no joy in Peninnah's sons and daughters: every infant cry, every child's laugh, every teenage voice around the home was like a knife piercing her, and Peninnah twisted and drove the knife home whenever she could. It was a thoroughly miserable home. It was all Elkanah's fault, of course, and unfortunately he was incapable of sorting it out.

National apostasy

But there was one other tragedy with which Hannah had to contend. It was a time of national backsliding, and religion was at a low ebb. Hophni and Phinehas were the sons of the high priest Eli, and they were godless and immoral. 'Ichabod' was written all over the land, the glory of the presence of God had departed from Israel. As the priests, so the people. It was a nation of bribery and extortion, of idolatry and violence. Hannah with her breaking heart, her emotional turmoil and her shattered home could turn nowhere in the nation to find true comfort. Nobody understood her: not in the home, nor in society, and not even at the place of worship—she was all alone with her grief.

Now, here was Hannah, standing in the tabernacle to pray: a lone and lonely woman praying in her heart to the only one who could hear and help her. Close by sat the ageing Eli, the high priest, who had his own family problems, and for very different reasons his heart must have been breaking also. He was struggling in vain to control his wild and lawless sons.

It was clearly so unusual to find a woman praying in the tabernacle, perhaps to find anyone praying in the tabernacle, that he took careful notice of her. And when he saw her lips moving and her face twisted with emotional pain, he assumed she was drunk. Even the high priest did not understand that Hannah was praying out of the bitterness of her soul.

It is not a happy picture. But it mirrors many Christians who are struggling with life in the same way: a problem, a bitterness, an anger, a resentment, finding it hard to come to terms with God and his ways. His plans seem far from good, acceptable and perfect. It seemed hardly fair that Peninnah, a woman with a hard and cruel heart and with little sympathetic blood running in her veins, should have all the children. Hannah's heart was that of a true mother, surely this is the one who should be having the children not the other one. Does God have it wrong?

Hannah's faith was God-centred and real

Hannah went up with her husband every year to worship at Shiloh, which at that time was the centre of religious life for the Israelites, since Jerusalem was not yet in their hands. She did not *have* to go with Elkanah because the Lord did not demand that the wife should accompany her husband; but she went nevertheless. Hannah went each year and each year as she went, her greatest desire was offered to God: 'In bitterness of soul Hannah wept much and prayed to the Lord' (v 10). In the Hebrew this reads better as, 'Hannah wept and prayed much to the Lord.' The little word 'much' covers both the praying and the weeping. She cried long and hard and she prayed long and hard.

Those two things are not contradictory. If we have a heart to pray, we can also have a heart to cry. Hannah knew that to cry about her problem was not a lack of trust or confidence, it was simply an expression of her emotion; that is what God had given her tears for. Tears when the heart is breaking are not a lack of faith, they are an expression of God-given human emotions. Animals do not cry in the way that humans do.

There is something very significant in Hannah's prayer. She made a vow that began, 'O Lord Almighty' (v 11). That phrase is used often in the Old Testament. The Hebrew is *yahweh tsaba* (literally 'Lord of hosts' or 'armies') and it occurs around two hundred and sixty times in the Old Testament, mainly in the words of the prophets. However, what is significant is that as a title for God is this the very first time it is recorded in prayer in the Old Testament. You will find its first use in verse 3, but that is not a prayer. The title appears nowhere in the Bible before this. It will be used hundreds of time later, but Hannah was the first recorded as using it to her God.

In Joshua 5:13 we have something similar. The same two words are there, but they are not used as a title of God. The man whom Joshua challenged outside the walls of Jericho with: 'Are you for us or for our enemies?' responded: 'As commander of the army of the Lord I have now come' (v 14). The phrase 'the army of the Lord' is *tsaba yahweh* in the Hebrew: 'the host of the Lord'; the same words, but not as a title for God.

The word *tsaba* is used, broadly speaking, in three ways in the Old Testament. It can refer to the armies of the nations; when the Midianites came out against Gideon they were described as the hosts stretched out in the valley. Secondly it is used of the stars in the heavens. But thirdly it refers to the inhabitants of heaven—the angelic hosts.

Here it is linked with the covenant name for the God of Israel—*Yahweh*. 'Lord' in our Old Testament translates the special name for God used only by the Jews. No other nation used it as a single title for their god. Many nations worshipped Baal, though often under different names, but no other nation worshipped Yahweh. It was a name that God had revealed to the Israelites through Moses (Exodus 3:14 and 6:6). To protect the name from being stolen or devalued by the nations, the Israelites would never pronounce it; instead, they substituted the normal word for a master of servants. In time the true pronunciation was lost, and to this day we cannot be sure of the correct pronunciation of *Yahweh*.

Thus, *Yahweh tsaba* was an exalted title used only for Israel's God, and it referred to his covenant-keeping promises as the God of the whole universe: the armies of nations, the stars in the sky and the hosts of angels. Perhaps this is the most exalted title of God in the Old Testament and it is surely a reference to our Lord Jesus Christ, for the covenant name of God points to the Son of God who came as the fulfilment of all God's promises for salvation and eternal security.

This title came first to the mind of Isaiah after his overwhelming vision of God in the temple: 'Woe to me! I am ruined! For I am a man of unclean lips, and I live among a people of unclean lips, and my eyes have seen the King, the Lord Almighty' (Isaiah 6:5). We know that this vision of *Yahweh tsaba* seen by Isaiah was of the Lord Jesus himself, because John comments in his Gospel, 'Isaiah said this because he saw Jesus' glory and spoke about him' (John 12:41). King David also used this expression when he thought of his God coming to his people in the tabernacle: 'Who is he, this King of glory? The Lord Almighty—He is the King of glory' (Psalm 24:10).

Yet it was Hannah, the mother of Samuel, who has left us the first record of this exalted phrase in prayer.

That was undoubtedly the secret of Hannah's faith—she held fast to a sovereign God in her chaotic circumstances: personally, domestically and nationally. She anticipated what Paul would later write about: 'In all things God works for the good of those who love him, who have been called according to his purpose'(Romans 8:28). Notice the introduction of that little word 'if' in 1 Samuel 1:11: 'O Lord Almighty, *if* you will only look upon your servant's misery and remember me.' Hannah would not presume to instruct God, she was prepared to leave the outcome in his hands and let him decide. That is a very wise thing to do.

However, we can look deeper into the prayer life of this woman, because after God had answered the prayer, she sang a beautiful hymn of praise to God (2:1–10). Here is an intimate reflection of her private relationship with God. What would people learn about our relationship with God if they listened in to our private, personal prayers?

Hannah did not expect this prayer to be read three thousand years later; it was between her and *Yahweh tsaba* alone. She described her God as holy and a Rock (v 2), as the one who knows (v 3), as the Lord of death and life (v 6) of poverty and wealth (v 7); he is the Creator (v 8), and the one who protects his people like a father (v 9), but can crush all those who oppose him (v 10). It must remind us of Mary's prayer recorded in Luke 1:46–55. Two of the most beautiful prayers in the Bible come from the lips of Hannah and Mary. Let mothers and grandmothers cultivate that personal walk with God. There would have been no Samuel without the prayers of Hannah, and she prayed for a son for the service of God. When Samuel came to the position of leadership after the death of old Eli, the nation was in a desperate state; yet, by the grace of God, revival came through the preaching and teaching of faithful Samuel—but remember who his mother was.

We can almost hear the indignation in her voice when Eli harshly accused her of being drunk (v 14). Hannah was not that kind of woman at all, and she wanted him to know it. She must have felt so bitterly disappointed because nobody understood her. I think she nearly broke poor old Eli's heart with her impassioned response to his accusation, because all he can find to say is, 'Go in peace.' And Hannah did not round on him but blessed him; what a beautiful character!

Hannah's faith was effective

Hannah 'wept and prayed' (v 10). We cannot underline this too much that tears show no lack of trust when the heart is breaking. We can weep and not pray, and we can pray and never learn how to weep, but this woman knew both. What is also significant is that she must have confidentially left her problem with God because without any evidence of an answer, Hannah went her way and ate something and 'her face was no longer downcast' (v 18). At that moment she had no more evidence that God would answer her prayer than she had when she first went into the tabernacle. And how often had she prayed a prayer similar to this? But now there was a strong confidence that all would be well. Her faith changed her life, there was a quiet and peaceful dignity now; joy became part of her expression.

When Samuel was born, Hannah's life was planned around the child. She had promised that she would give the child back to God in the service of the Lord, and when, the next year, Elkanah made plans to go up to Shiloh once again, Hannah declined to join him, preferring to care for the child in the few years that she had before her promise must be fulfilled. Hannah had only one purpose in view in that time: the service that Samuel would give to God. Hannah was a mother who was faithful in praying for her child.

The following words were written in the diary of a mother in Long Island, America around the year 1809: 'This morning I rose very early to pray for my children and especially that my sons may be ministers and missionaries for Christ.' That mother had five sons and three daughters. All five sons became missionaries or ministers and one of the daughters was Harriet Beecher Stowe who wrote the book *Uncle Toms' Cabin* which beautifully illustrated the gospel of Christ and was so influential in exposing the horrors of the American slave trade; it played a significant part in the final abolition of slavery across North America. William Havergal, the father of Frances Ridley Havergal the hymn writer, wrote on the death of his mother in 1850: 'I feel that I have lost my praying mother.' A few years ago I lost *my* praying mother in her mid-nineties and, after the death of my wife Barbara, she was my best prayer partner. We can never underestimate the value of the prayers of mothers and grandmothers. The lack of that undoubtedly explains a current generation of wild, lawless and lost children.

Hannah's faith was faithful

As we would expect, Hannah was full of joy to the Lord (2:1), but for all her joy, she never forgot her promise. She called the child Samuel. It is not quite true to say that the name means 'heard of God', because it was a name that Hannah made up. There was nobody else called Samuel before Samuel, and the Hebrew word does not mean 'heard of God'. Hannah gave him that name because in the Hebrew it *sounded like* the phrase 'heard of God'. In technical jargon it is assonance rather than etymology that determined her choice of a name—in other words, what it sounded like rather than what it actually meant. Hannah invented a name as a perpetual reminder that her God heard and answered her prayer.

Hannah had an honest faith, and the family would always know that she would keep her word and carry through anything she began for God; this was an example that would help Samuel in years to come. When he later reminded King Saul that obedience is better than sacrifice (1 Samuel 15:22–23), that was a lesson he himself had learned from his mother. Children see a lot more of their mothers than their fathers and they need to see a consistent faith.

Jane Campbell, the mother of Duncan Campbell who was so greatly used of God on the Western Isles of Scotland in revival in the 1940s and 50s, was known for her worship and honour of God even with the increasing activity of her family around her. Duncan Campbell's biographer writes that she was undoubtedly the greatest influence in his life. From the moment of her conversion we are told she walked consistently with the Saviour and she lived a beautiful Christ-like life in front of her children. In her, the children found a friend in whom they could confide and it was said that her knowledge of the Scriptures was so full, that masculine pride took a beating when it came to arguments about theological issues over the Bible. Jane Campbell had a wonderful gift of unravelling the mysteries of grace. She never went very far from home, but like a magnet she attracted people to her. Duncan Campbell's biographer comments that she lived and loved and prayed until in old age, after much suffering, with the Bible still propped up before her and the heavenly light glowing on her face, she fell asleep in Jesus. Duncan Campbell never forgot the debt that he owed to his mother.

Hannah's faith was sacrificial

What Hannah took for her first sacrifice at the tabernacle (1:24), was more than was required. According to the Law, all that was demanded of her for the first-born son was a lamb, or for the very poor even pigeons would be sufficient. Any other offering was the maximum of a bull for the whole family. That was what Hannah took: an offering for the whole family. Samuel saw in his mother a faith that cost her. In addition, she had promised Samuel back to the Lord. The promise that 'no razor will ever be used on his head' (v 11) was a reference to the Nazarite vow, the rules for which are set out in Numbers 6. Hannah was familiar with this and would train her son for a lifetime of service to God.

The statement 'After he was weaned' (v 24) may at first appear shocking! We imagine a toddler being taken from his mother and cast into the service of the tabernacle miles from home. It was not quite like that. The weaned child is one who is becoming independent of his mother, and this is confirmed by the word used of Samuel in the phrase 'she took the boy with her'. Hebrew is rich in its words for children, and there are eight separate words that describe the child from the womb to 'the ripened one' who leaves home. The word that is used here is *naar* which refers to 'the one who shakes himself free' and it is better translated as a young man or youth. But it was still a wrench for her.

A mother's purpose is to train her children to leave the home. She must let them go and not resent or begrudge it. In the spring there are little fledglings in nests all over the country. What if the hen refused to allow her fledglings to leave the nest? The whole fulfilment of her task is to get them out into the big world and strong enough to survive. That is precisely where too many mothers in our nation fail today.

Anyone who knows anything of the story of Samuel will be aware of the little coat that Hannah made for her son each year. We can imagine her tears and prayers as she wove it and carefully sewed it together. That coat was for Samuel a reminder of his mother's love and prayers. Every time he put it on he knew that his mother was praying for him. Her tears and her fears followed him daily because she knew only too well the kind of company he was forced to mix with. Eli's sons were wicked men (2:12–17). They had no regard for the Lord and were treating the Lord's offering with contempt. They were, supposedly, his role models. It is not hard to sense the emphasis of the very next sentence: 'But Samuel was ministering before the

Lord' (v 18). Against that background, how on earth did Samuel stand? Back at home, his mother was praying.

And the Lord rewarded Hannah for her commitment (v 21), and she had three sons and two daughters. She who once was barren had six children in all. But she never forgot her commitment to Samuel. Mothers well understand this constant care. Children leave home and marry, but a mother is not sure that she worries about them less than when they were toddlers in the home. I heard of the elderly lady in her mid-nineties who declared to a visitor at her care home that she was now ready to go to the Lord because she had seen the last of her sons safely installed in an old people's home!

1 Samuel 2:21 is the last reference to Hannah by name in the entire Bible. She passes from the pages of history with no more mention; but that would not have bothered her any more than it bothered any of God's little people. It was her son Samuel that she prayed for and this was the name that would continue. Hannah's value was seen in him.

Abigail—A gentle answer turns away wrath

'My lord, let the blame be on me alone' 1 Samuel 25:24

We live in an incredible world of technology. Thanks to Intel, you can buy a surf-board with a built-in PC so that while surfing the waves you can also surf the net, take photos and send emails. With an H2o audio SV-iPod, you can relax in the pool—and even swim under water—whilst listening to your favourite music. More mundane is the fact that for some time now we have been able to buy a powerful memory stick that will double as a key ring fob and will store all your family and holiday pictures, so that you can simply plug it into your friends' laptop and bore them for hours with all your treasured pictures on full screen. It is all very clever—but as the media headlines constantly remind us, clever people cannot always control their emotions.

Back in 1969, Neil Armstrong and Buzz Aldrin were the first men to step onto the lunar surface, but when they came back, so the story goes, there were no still photos of Armstrong on the moon. The reason? Aldrin was so mad at his colleague for taking the privilege of being the first man on the moon that he took no stills of him as a payback. Clever people, gone mad. Politicians and presidents have forfeited a nation's respect and loyalty for just 'a moment of madness'.

This is one reason why we need the Bible. It is full of stories about people; but they are not merely stories for our entertainment, they are there to teach us vital lessons—lessons to do with life. Many of these stories introduce us to what I call: 'God's little people'—those who appear briefly on the pages of the Bible and yet seem to play no major part in the great scheme of the plan of redemption. They are, like most of us, little people who fit into God's plan somewhere.

There are few Old Testament stories more powerful and few characters more beautiful than that which is contained in the single chapter about

Abigail. In this story we have some valuable lessons on the danger of losing self-control—and of how to deal with it in other people.

David was holed up in the wilderness of Paran with the spies of Saul watching his every move and always waiting for an opportunity to pounce. Knowing that God had rejected him because of his disobedience, Saul knew also that the future of the monarchy lay in the hands of this shepherd boy and giant killer from Bethlehem. For his part, David was a hunted outlaw whose natural command of men had first gained him high military rank over the armies of Saul, and then, when he fell from favour, had gathered around him a band of malcontents. It is doubtful whether that was ever his intention, but many who, for good reason and bad, were under threat in their community, took this as their opportunity to head for the hills:

David left Gath and escaped to the cave of Adullam. When his brothers and his father's household heard about it, they went down to him there. All those who were in distress or in debt or discontented gathered round him, and he became their leader. About four hundred men were with him (1 Samuel 22:1–2).

We can understand David's family joining him, because Bethlehem was just twelve miles to the north east of Adullam, and Saul had already included the name of Jesse in his murderous threats against David (20:31); they perhaps reasonably guessed that the king would either hold them to ransom or take revenge on them. David himself must have been surprised at the swelling numbers that almost immediately joined him in exile. The four hundred soon grew to six hundred. Among them were undoubtedly some good men, but equally certainly, a significant number of rogues took advantage of the security in numbers. It turned out to be a small army of desperate and determined men, many of whom were angry and bitter. Perhaps no questions were asked of the daily influx of new recruits, and if they were, no story could be checked. The same word that is used to describe them, 'bitter in soul', is used of Hannah's desperate prayer (1:10) and Job's despondent cry (Job 3:20), whilst in Judges 18:25 the rabble from the tribe of Dan are described with the same word as 'angry'.

So, a mixed band of honest men who perhaps had fallen out of favour with the bad-tempered king or were victims of community gossip, mingled with thieves, rogues, ne'er-do-wells and those with grudges, old scores and feuds to settle. A generally unattractive mob—and over these David quickly asserted leadership and control.

The 'cave' of Adullam was more likely a 'mountain stronghold' (the word *metsadah* is found also as the last in the list in Judges 6:2 where it is translated as 'stronghold'). A 'cave' is *chur* (and that is the second to last word in Judges 6:2). The meaning of 'Adullam' is uncertain, but it may refer to a place of retreat. David thoughtfully persuaded the king of Moab to allow his ageing parents to live safely in his territory; the constant movement of an exile was no life for them. It was here in the mountain stronghold of Adullam, that David received the terrible news that Saul had slaughtered eighty-five priests from the city of Nob because Abimelech had innocently provided David with food and a weapon. There would be little mercy for David and his men if the king got hold of them. The resolve of the exiles was stiffened: they had everything to lose if they showed weakness.

The next few months (or years?) saw David and his men constantly on the move, under surveillance and under threat; David could never be certain who among his motley crew might betray him for a royal reward. In the wilderness of Ziph they were under daily danger from the far larger army of Saul, and the small remnant were forced to keep moving from place to place (23:13). By this time they had been in some of the most barren and desolate landscape falling down to the Dead Sea. It was a cruel and inhospitable area with little or nothing to offer by way of food, whether natural or cultivated. Ziph is now a 'ruin mound' some 2,880 feet above the Sea, and four miles south east of Hebron.

Saul's son and David's best friend, Jonathan, maintained a secret line of communication with David, and when he found David here at Ziph he 'helped him to find strength in God' (23:16). David certainly needed this, because when next we catch up with him and his men they are in the wilderness of Maon (v 24), an area described by one traveller as 'waste pasture-land, rough rocks with that dry vegetation on which goats and even sheep seem to thrive'. By the end of 1 Samuel 23 David is in the 'strongholds of En Gedi', and at last they were in more hospitable territory where wild goats seemed abundant and sheep were being farmed (24:3). Here, David spared the life of Saul, and his absolute authority over his men is significant in the light of this incredible opportunity to kill their hated enemy.

All this is not merely introductory but essential to the point at which our story has arrived. With Saul off his back for a moment—presumably chastened by David's merciful behaviour and preoccupied with the necessary mourning for the death of the prophet Samuel (25:1)—David could move a little more freely; and he and his men had the opportunity to slip into the far more fertile region of Carmel—a broad, pleasant and fruitful land. This is not the Mount Carmel we are more familiar with; that was situated some one hundred miles to the north west. In Joshua 15:55 Carmel is linked with Maon and Ziph in the hill country in the south. It is not hard to imagine that after such a rigorous period of eking out an existence in barren wildernesses, the high fertile plain of Carmel must have offered 'manna from heaven'. What made it all the more attractive was the fact there was at least one very wealthy landowner in the area with no fewer than three thousand sheep and a thousand goats. He lived in the mountain city of Maon.

With such a temptation in front of him and with such a gang behind him, David was in a strong position to steal or demand a few animals for his men at any time; it would save the trouble of foraging for their own meals among the fleet-footed animals on the rocky ranges around them. So, when David passed out the order that there was to be no looting from the locals, his men must have thought he was mad to let such an opportunity pass them by. First he allowed his bitter enemy to escape, and now he passed up free meals for all. Doubtless they respected his leadership, though questioned his judgement.

However, David clearly refused to allow his men to take anything that they did not pay for. More than this, the order also went out that the local shepherds were not only not to be molested, but they were to be protected from bandits or wild animals wherever possible. The later evidence of the shepherds was eloquent testimony both to David's integrity and to his firm command of his men (1 Samuel 25:14–16).

What David did not know, was that the owner of this vast flock grazing so temptingly across the fertile plain, was 'surly and mean' in all his dealings; he also appears to have owned a sharp tongue and a very hot temper. He was clearly a greedy glutton and bad-tempered drunkard and had little care for anyone but himself. He was a descendant of Caleb (v 3), a faithful ancestry, since Caleb and Joshua were the only two spies who, in the time of Moses, had confidence in God—a godly ancestry is no guarantee for the present generation.

In fact, Nabal had only one significant credit to his name—he had a wife who was beautiful in every respect. How sweet Abigail became wedded to such a boor as Nabal, we cannot now know. Perhaps she was a child bride or it was an arranged marriage? We can hardly imagine her falling in love with him—the story reveals that she had far too much common sense for that!

Enter Abigail

The story in chapter 25 is packed with the drama of two men's anger and passion out of control; it is the account of the lack of wisdom and intemperate thought that comes to men whose temper explodes—both David and Nabal. We are brought to an apparent climax with David, slighted and insulted by this mean and selfish landowner, breathing vengeance and slaughter even on the very men he had so recently been protecting. Then, dramatically, in the central point of the story, when wholesale massacre is pending, all becomes calm and rational—enter Abigail.

David's request of Nabal seemed perfectly reasonable. It was the normal custom to celebrate this 'harvest' of sheep shearing with a feast, at which gifts would be given away to the poor and to strangers. David's men had never stolen anything that belonged to Nabal, they did not harm the shepherds and on the contrary they had proved to be a wall of protection to them; since David clearly had the upper hand in strength and numbers, it was an evidence of his integrity that nothing would be done dishonestly to the property of Nabal.

The young men sent by David are courteous—the large number of ten messengers was not intended as a threat but in that culture was a mark of respect for Nabal's importance—and at the end they waited ('sat down' would be more accurate), again a mark of respect. The details of what would be an acceptable gift in return is not specified (25:5–8); that is left to Nabal's generosity. However, generosity did not figure in the vocabulary of this mean-spirited man.

It is inconceivable that Nabal did not know of David, since the whole nation was talking about him, and his military prowess had entered the folksongs of the people (18:7), so much so that even the neighbouring Philistines had picked it up (21:10–11). It could be argued that Nabal feared for his own life if he aided an outlaw; but if this was in his mind he could have given this as his reason for refusal and, in the light of the tragic experience of the priests of Nob (chapter 22), had he done so we may have given him some credit. On the contrary, Nabal appears to have been so wrapped up in his own 'little money changing hole' that he was unconcerned for the big events happening around him.

Unlike his wife, he was totally indifferent to the work of Samuel and the prophecies concerning David. It is unlikely that any parents would have named their child Nabal, which means 'fool', so this was almost certainly the common nickname that he was given to express most people's contempt for his utter stupidity. His response is to level David with any other runaway slave—overlooking the testimony of his own shepherds indicating that David was not an ordinary bandit or desperado.

Apparently David had sent trusted men on this forlorn mission, because they were careful to report 'every word' back to their leader. In response, Nabal poured out an invective designed to mock and belittle David as much as he could (v 14). When David received the reply, he exploded! If Nabal's response was unreasonable, David's was inexcusable. In a blind rage he called out his men and headed up to the farm.

It is at this point of high drama that Abigail entered the story. We can imagine the servants clustering around her, whom they clearly respect as a wise and caring woman; they pour out the story of David's protection and then blurt out their assessment of Nabal: 'He is such a wicked man that no one can talk to him' (v 17). They clearly knew that they could speak this freely to Abigail, and one wonders how often they had used her gentle wisdom to defuse problems in the past.

Abigail wasted no time loading donkeys and headed down towards David's little army. When finally the two parties met, David was still raging about the insult from Nabal (vs 21–22). But worse, he now threatened—with oaths to back it up—that he would kill every man belonging to this mean landowner. This meant that scores of completely innocent men would be massacred—men whom he had recently protected. If David had carried out this threat, it would have placed him in exactly the same category as the butchery of Saul on the innocent priests of Nob and it would have given credence to the accusation of Saul that he was a trouble-maker in the kingdom. A lot was at stake in how this story would turn out.

If ever there was an example of 'A wife of noble character ... worth far more than rubies' (Proverbs 31:10), it would be found in Abigail. King Lemuel wrote of the perfect wife in this way:

She is clothed with strength and dignity ... She speaks with wisdom, and faithful instruction is on her tongue. She watches over the affairs of her household and does not eat the bread of idleness. Her children arise and call her blessed (Proverbs 31:25–28).

Sadly, in this case Lemuel misjudged a man like Nabal when he concluded: 'her husband also, and he praises her.' But observe how Abigail handled this desperate situation.

The army was on the way, and once the massacre began, the blood of the young men would be hot with killing and it would be far too late for anyone to intervene. But there was no panic in Abigail's response. I see her calmly ordering the servants—who are in increasing terror as the moments pass—to gather and load the food that David's men need and deserve. She 'lost no time', but neither did she act impulsively; all that she did was wisely and carefully measured. Where would she find: 'two hundred loaves of bread, two skins of wine, five dressed sheep, five seahs of roasted grain, a hundred cakes of raisins and two hundred cakes of pressed figs' (v 18)? Clearly they were part of the extravagant, 'royal' banquet prepared on the orders of Nabal for that very night (v 36). Abigail was not slow in seeing this as a providence of God. At such a banquet, perhaps this amount would not be missed; more likely, as she mounted her donkey, she left orders for the servants to replace what she had taken.

Wisely, she did not tell her husband, but had every intention of doing so at the right time—most astute wives know when that 'right' time comes. The gifts are sent on ahead as a first step of appeasement, but what follows in the story tells us all that we need to know about the beautiful character of Abigail. She well earned the commendation of verse 3 that she was intelligent, and the same word is found in Proverbs 16:22, '*Understanding* is a fountain of life to those who have it, but folly brings punishment to fools.'

At what point Abigail got up from her knees in the dust before David we do not know, however, what is clear is that she dared to preach a little sermon to this mighty warrior. In fact it was a sermon with no less than six points. She reminded David of his anger, his God, his men, his future, his conscience and finally his servant—Abigail herself.

'Let the blame be on me alone' (v 24)

It is Abigail's very first words that impress us most of all: 'My lord, let the blame be on me alone.' At that moment Abigail placed the lives of all the estate servants above her own. She placed herself as a sacrificial lamb between two violently angry men and offered herself as an atonement. It was reminiscent of Moses who, when Israel had made themselves an Apis bull to worship, pleaded with God: 'Please forgive their sin—but if not, then blot me out of the book you have written' (Exodus 32:32). Moses would exchange his eternal life for the sake of the nation. Abigail was made of the same heartfelt compassion. As a woman she was not included in David's bloodthirsty oath, it was only the men who would die; but Abigail would sell her life to rescue the servants, shepherds and herdsmen.

Both Moses and Abigail are, in effect, pictures of the great Mediator who gave his life on behalf of all who are called according to his purpose. But unlike Moses and Abigail who offered their lives on behalf of others, and whose offer was not taken up, Christ offered his life and the Father accepted it as the price for our redemption: 'For there is one God and one mediator between God and men, the man Christ Jesus, who gave himself as a ransom for all men' (1 Timothy 2:5).

Writing to the Christians at Philippi, Paul urged them each to express a humility that placed others above themselves (Philippians 2:3). That is precisely what Abigail did. And that was guaranteed to stop David in his tracks! Such humility usually has that effect on the railing of an ill-tempered world. Abigail has bared her neck to the sword of David and the heat of his rage began to cool: 'A gentle answer turns away wrath' (Proverbs 15:1).

Now Abigail began to reason. She admitted the folly of her husband's action, and if we consider her to be disloyal to Nabal, we must remember the kind of man he undoubtedly was and all that was at stake at this moment—if David brushed her aside at this moment, scores of lives would be lost. The word fool (*nabal* in Hebrew, v 25) was not a word that Abigail would use flippantly; it referred to someone who, in the words of our Lord in the parable: 'neither feared God nor cared about men' (Luke 18:2). The word is employed in Isaiah 32:5–6 where the character of Nabal is perfectly described:

No longer will the fool be called noble nor the scoundrel be highly respected. For the fool speaks folly, his mind is busy with evil: He practises ungodliness and spreads error concerning the Lord; the hungry he leaves empty and from the thirsty he withholds water.

There could be no better description of Nabal's action than this.

Abigail took David's side and she let him know that she understood why he was so angry. However—and she needed to buy time while David cooled down—if only the young men had come to *her* with their request, the outcome would have been very different, as the gifts demonstrate. More than this, Abigail implied that David should not stoop to the level of taking a fool seriously: 'Do not answer a fool according to his folly, or you will be like him yourself' (Proverbs 26:4). Frankly, there are some people who are hardly worth arguing with; still less is it worth defending one's reputation against them.

Her plea for forgiveness for 'your servant's offence' (v 28) may refer to her husband, though since he was not interested in forgiveness, and since Abigail had already taken the blame upon herself, the reference is most likely to herself. If she had her husband in mind, it was a powerful reminder to David that, as one commentator has expressed it: 'a wise man should pardon a fool.' Showing mercy surely comes more easily when we realize that the offender is a fool. If the reference is to herself, then the plea is for total forgiveness. We need not debate the facts that mercy rather than forgiveness was more appropriate for Nabal, or that her attempt at surrogate guilt and blame was really not possible; we are concerned for her mind and heart, both of which tell us that she was a humble and spiritual woman in touch with God.

'The Lord has kept you from bloodshed' (v 26)

At this point, the little ambassador felt she could step up the pressure on this fierce warrior towering over her. She brought the name of the Lord into the plea. That was something David had only done in the form of his rash oath of murderous intention (v 22). But he had left the Lord out at his peril, and someone had to tell him. Her cool reasoning and sound theology led her to the conclusion that all the circumstances that brought Abigail and this giant killer face to face, were nothing less than the providence of the covenant God of Israel: 'The Lord has kept you from bloodshed' (v 26). It is the mark of a spiritual woman when she can see the hand of God in all the circumstances of life; she knew now what David would learn to appreciate more fully, that God sees all our going out and lying down and is familiar with all our ways (Psalm 139:3).

Perhaps Abigail did not yet know that David had so generously spared the life of Saul in the desert of En Gedi (chapter 24); there, the future king stood tall in his honourable integrity and merciful spirit—the moral high ground was his; he was even conscience stricken for having cut off the corner of Saul's cloak (24:5). But now he was as shabby and mean as the man he was about to kill. That is what mindless revenge always does to us; vengeance drags us to the level of those who have wronged us.

David did not need to wait nine hundred years until Paul penned these words to the Christians at Rome: 'Do not take revenge, my friends, but leave room for God's wrath, for it is written: "It is mine to avenge; I will repay," says the Lord' (Romans 12:19); it was already written in the law of Moses, which David knew well (Deuteronomy 32:35).

However, the best example of all is the Lord himself. When Peter was encouraging the young Christians to bear up under unjust punishment, he reminded them:

To this you were called, because Christ suffered for you, leaving you an example, that you should follow in his steps. 'He committed no sin, and no deceit was found in his mouth.' When they hurled their insults at him, he did not retaliate; when he suffered, he made no threats. Instead, he entrusted himself to him who judges justly (1 Peter 2:21–23).

A bitter spirit of revenge can always justify itself, which is precisely what

David was doing as he charged in a blind rage into the ravine rehearsing to himself the good reasons for his action (vs 21–22). But thank God for the cool wisdom and calm words of a woman whose confidence that she could turn events is seen in her bold prophecy that the Lord has already 'kept you, my master, from bloodshed and from avenging yourself with your own hands' (v 26).

'Let this gift be given to the men who follow you' (v 27)

There is a subtlety about Abigail's presentation of the food and drink that should not be overlooked. The amount would hardly sustain an army of six hundred for long; it was intended as a token of her intention, but it was offered to David for his men and not for him alone—a reminder that his primary responsibility was the welfare of his men and not his own dented pride. That too was a wise move and the emphasis of her words may not have been lost on David.

He had been given the task, though unsought, of caring for a desperate band of outlaws. They had generally obeyed his orders and followed his leadership. By his example of integrity he had shown them all a better way of living than many of them had been accustomed to. Sharing and unselfishness was a lesson he was already beginning to teach his men, and would do so more in the future (compare 25:13 with 30:24). This was a leader who cared for them and whom they could respect. Many of them would follow David through thick and thin in the future. But now, suddenly, in a fit of selfish rage, all that was thrown to the wind. This one moment of madness would never be forgotten and from now on his men would learn a lesson that morality was fine until it cut across your personal pride. Abigail understood all this so well and therefore reminded him in a simple way of his responsibility to the men who followed him. What lessons are they now learning from his actions?

No man ever sins to himself alone. There are always others watching, whether our children, church members, students, colleagues, employees, neighbours or friends. David had forgotten the big picture in a moment of focussing on his own petty quarrel—and that is where most church bickering starts. Is the example to the world and the unity of the church more important that our personal pride? How many men—politicians especially—live to regret their moment of uncontrolled emotion.

'The Lord will make a lasting dynasty for my master' (v 28)

The reference to God hurling away David's enemies 'as from the pocket of a sling' (v 29) was smart! It was calculated to tell David that this woman was well aware of his military triumph at the beginning, and how it came about. Perhaps, at this point, David began to smile. Here was a rerun of David and Goliath, but now David was a brave little woman kneeling before him in the dirt—and her sling was every bit on target as his had been. David was listening, so Abigail pressed home her advantage.

Clearly she was aware of the events of the nation and that David stood tall in the outcome of those events. Abigail revealed that she knew David would one day become king in Israel, and by implication—'Even though someone is pursuing you to take your life' (v 29)—she let him know that she was well aware of what he and his men had been through in recent months. But had David forgotten that 'The life of my master will be bound securely in the bundle of the living by the Lord your God' (v 29)? Here was an appeal to his theology. Had David not seen the incredible deliverance from the Lord on so many occasions recently? Had he forgotten so quickly? Could not this intervention by such an unworthy little woman be just another example of God's providence?

We can hardly doubt that even if Nabal could find no time to mourn the death of Samuel, Abigail certainly did. She seemed to be well aware of the promises of God that had come through Samuel (v 30) and she had no doubt that all those promises would lead to David becoming king over Israel. We cannot know how she could be aware of the promises to David, because what took place in 1 Samuel 16 was a private family affair, but this spiritual woman with her 'ear to the ground' of what really mattered in Israel, knew very well all that was prepared by the Lord for David. Nevertheless her statement: 'The Lord will make a lasting dynasty for my master … and has appointed him leader over Israel' (vs 28,30) was a massive claim of faith, because already there were tensions between Israel in the north and Judah in the south, and these would come to the fore when David eventually succeeded Saul, and they surfaced to the point of an irrevocable split when David's son, Solomon, died. Abigail could not possibly know all this, but she knew that the kingdom was promised to David and she had no doubt that what God promised, he would deliver.

Abigail was equally sure that the life that was prophesied would be protected. There was no doubt in her mind that her God was in sovereign control over the life of all his chosen people. The phrase 'the bundle of the living' referred to the custom of binding valuable items carefully and tightly so that they would not be lost or damaged. If only, in every circumstance of life, we could believe that 'all things work together for good for those who are called according to his purpose' (Romans 8:28 ESV)—and if only we would always act upon that belief.

'The staggering burden of needless bloodshed' (v 31)

And now came the final thrust of her rapier words: When God has done for you everything that he has promised, do you want to have on your conscience such a terrible act as this proposed massacre? Abigail described it as 'the staggering burden of needless bloodshed' (v 31). Someone has noted that 'Wicked vows are ill made but worse kept'. Such a powerful argument totally won over David, and every man's sword was already being sheathed.

Now, at last, David brought the Lord into his response and seems to have recognized the enormity and unreasonableness of his proposed action: 'Praise be the Lord the God of Israel, who has sent you today to meet me' (v 32). His had not been an act of defence in the course of the Lord's battles, but rather it was the heated and irrational response of a man who has been slighted and whose pride has been mauled. David thought that in the sight of his men he must show himself strong and that it was 'manly' to defend his honour. It took a woman to show him otherwise.

Every day of every year, on every continent and in every nation, quarrels break out, families break up and lives are taken, only because someone wants personal revenge to defend their name or reputation. Every year, thousands of men, in a moment of hurt pride, strike out to defend what they think is their honour, and as a result they become common criminals confined for years, often for life, within prison walls. That is how it has been throughout the history of the human race. Abigail is a history lesson for a better and wiser path.

Sadly, where was Abigail when, many years later, David lusted for another woman and committed the double sin of adultery and murder?

How he needed her then. A 'good conscience towards God' (1 Peter 3:21) is worth a fortune in this world's goods. But when we have failed to hear the wisdom of Abigail and have fallen into sin, 'How much more, then, will the blood of Christ, who through the eternal Spirit offered himself unblemished to God, cleanse our consciences from acts that lead to death, so that we may serve the living God!' (Hebrews 9:14).

'Intelligent, beautiful and good judgement' (vs 3,33)

When Abigail made her final plea: 'remember your servant' (v 31), David was now as quick to commend Abigail and listen to her common sense as he had been to plan revenge on the house of Nabal. That at least speaks well of David. But it speaks far louder in the praise of Abigail.

There are three words describing Abigail in this story, but unfortunately they do not always fit together in the same woman. She was described as 'intelligent and beautiful' in v.3 and as having 'good judgement' in v 33. The first word refers to her wisdom or understanding, the second to her physical loveliness, and the third to her discretion or sound judgement. The fact that the last two are by no means always found together is humorously illustrated for us in Proverbs: 'Like a gold ring in a pig's snout is a beautiful woman who shows no discretion' (11:22).

When, in the New Testament, Peter encouraged the Christian wives to win their husbands to Christ, he held before them the example of 'the holy women of the past who put their hope in God'. He had Sarah, Abraham's wife, especially in mind, but he might just as easily have been thinking of Abigail:

Your beauty should not come from outward adornment, such as braided hair and the wearing of gold jewellery and fine clothes. Instead, it should be that of your inner self, the unfading beauty of a gentle and quiet spirit, which is of great worth in God's sight. For this is the way the holy women of the past who put their hope in God used to make themselves beautiful (1 Peter 3:3–5).

Physical good looks is something that a woman can do little about, though she can take comfort in the fact that 'beauty is in the eye of the beholder' and not all men have the same template of attractiveness in mind! But every

Christian woman can make it a matter of prayer and diligent application to gain spiritual intelligence and discretion; in other words to possess a large portion of Abigail's wisdom.

A gentle word, a little thought, quiet reasoning, and a soft response is all that is so often needed in the home, at church and in the office or classroom to defuse a potentially explosive situation; a slanging match never has a winner. The proverb is so right and is beautifully illustrated in the story of Abigail:

A gentle answer turns away wrath, but a harsh word stirs up anger. The tongue of the wise commends knowledge, but the mouth of the fool gushes folly (Proverbs 15:1–2).

But our commendation of Abigail is not quite ended. David took the gifts she had brought, promised that she and the whole estate would be spared, and encouraged her to go home 'in peace'. She certainly needed that final blessing! To break the news of her actions to Nabal would require even greater tact and discretion than she displayed in approaching David. Here was the mark of a submissive wife. Did she need to tell Nabal and risk his terrible anger? But her balance of responsibility was exactly right: she would disobey his ungodly action and rebuttal of David, but she would then own up to what she had done.

For his part, the fool does not seem to have missed her at his banquet; doubtless he was too taken up acting as 'mine host' to miss such a triviality as his wife! By the time Abigail arrived home, the party was well under way and, as usual, Nabal was already worse for his drink. Wisely, Abigail concluded that this was not the time to own up to her actions. Perhaps she feared his violent reaction when he was 'in high spirits and very drunk' (v 36) or else she reasoned that he would hardly be likely to understand what she was telling him. Either way, Abigail kept her counsel until the morning.

When the news was broken 'his heart failed him and he became like a stone' (v 37). This is generally taken to be a description of a stroke, which is hardly surprising when we consider the surfeit of rich food and strong alcohol of the night before, combined with the shock of realizing the immediate danger that he had been in, and the humiliating actions of his wife. It was enough to finish any man with a temperament like his. Within ten days he was dead—and the Scripture does not hesitate to see this as a fulfilment of his wife's own prophecy recorded in verse 29: 'The Lord struck Nabal and he died' (v 38).

Happily this is not quite the end of the story, for David, hearing of Nabal's death and remembering what a jewel of a woman Abigail was, not only praised God once more for her wisdom and the fact that God had vindicated him, but he sent messengers asking if she would become his wife. Her deep humility had not changed even though she now had proved herself capable of influencing the most powerful man around, and who was now courting her. The response recorded in verse 41 is not to be dismissed as merely eastern culture, this was what we have come to expect of Abigail. She was consistently humble, knew her responsibility to acknowledge the headship of her future husband, and willingly placed herself at God's disposal. It would be risky, trading an estate for the life of an outlaw.

Someone has concluded: 'Only a woman could have managed such a negotiation as this so smoothly and successfully.' Perhaps, but how many bitter disputes with tragic conclusions could have been avoided in the history of Christian churches and families, not to mention the world beyond, if people had taken the trouble to learn from Abigail, the widow of Nabal and the wife of David?

Perhaps her example is one of the best illustrations we will find of Peter's claim that, 'love covers over a multitude of sins' (1 Peter 4:8), which is reinforced by James: 'Whoever turns a sinner from the error of his way will save him from death and cover over a multitude of sins' (James 5:20).

Three thousand years on we live in an age of technology that would have been unimaginable to Abigail—but she has left us an example of wisdom and a beautiful character that is a thousand times more worthwhile than the latest scientific piece of magic.

The widow of Zarephath— the best of faith

'There were many widows in Israel … Yet Elijah was not sent to any of them, but to a widow in Zarephath' Luke 4:25–26

In his record of the life of Christ, John Mark left us the story of an incident that took place when the Lord was in the vicinity of Tyre (Mark 7:24–30). A Syro-Phoenician mother brought her daughter to Jesus to be healed from an evil spirit. The test of her faith, and her confident response: 'Even the dogs under the table eat the children's crumbs', is well told and well known. It was in the same vicinity of Tyre that another story of one of God's little women is situated. In fact, Jesus referred to it in a highly significant comment recorded in Luke 4:24–26.

Early in his ministry he had been teaching in his home town of Nazareth. It was hardly an encouraging start because although 'all spoke well of him and were amazed at the gracious words that came from his lips', he was finally run out of town by the Jews and only escaped with his life because he alone would choose the time and manner of his death, and not others. What upset the synagogue worshippers in Nazareth was his reference to two events in the Hebrew Scriptures which illustrated God's gracious care for those outside Israel. Jesus described the first like this: 'I assure you that there were many widows in Israel in Elijah's time, when the sky was shut for three and a half years and there was a severe famine throughout the land. Yet Elijah was not sent to any of them, but to a widow in Zarephath in the region of Sidon.'

That infuriated the leaders in Nazareth, and well it might. The story he referred to took place some eight hundred and seventy years earlier in the time of Ahab, king of Israel. After the death of Solomon, his son Rehoboam took over the throne and stupidly caused a division in the kingdom which meant that ten tribes hived off to form their own separate kingdom in the north of the country, leaving just two tribes, Judah and Benjamin, in the south. The northern kingdom was called Israel, and over the first fifty-six years of its history, up to the accession of Ahab, it was ruled by six kings—all bad—and Ahab, as the seventh, was worse than any of the others. Ahab lived in a brand-new city called Samaria, built by his father Omri (1 Kings 16:24), and that became the capital of the northern kingdom for the next one hundred and fifty years.

Chief among Ahab's evil was the fact that he married the infamous Jezebel, the daughter of the king of Sidon. At this time Sidon, and in fact the whole of this Mediterranean coast, was under the control of Assyria, and Sidon sent an annual tribute to Ashurnasirpal II of Assyria. When Jezebel arrived in Israel as the wife of Ahab, she encouraged the already entrenched worship of Baal who was the God of storm, master of the earth, and son of Dagon (see 1 Samuel 5:1–5); Jezebel's father's name was Ethbaal. She also encouraged the worship of the Asherah (the goddess of fertility and Mother of All).

In addition, Jezebel must certainly have introduced the worship of a god, not mentioned in the Bible, but who for at least a thousand years had been the principal deity of this whole area along the Mediterranean seaboard. The name of this god was Eshmun and, significantly for our story, he was the god of health and healing. Eshmun had a consort called Eshmunit, and a temple dedicated to her has been discovered. Eshmun was known as 'The Holy Prince' and his symbol was a snake coiled round a rod or a snake biting its own tail and thus forming a circle, a symbol of eternity. The principal temple for his worship was located in the city of Jezebel's birth, Sidon—just eight miles north of a little village called Zarephath, referred to by Jesus nearly nine hundred years later in his sermon at Nazareth; Zarephath straddled the direct link from Sidon to Tyre.

At the time of our story, Israel was at a desperately low ebb spiritually—not that it had been anything other since the split with Judah in the south. A godless king was on the throne and he was married to an idol worshipper of the most cruel and debased kind who introduced her gods and goddesses to the worship of Israel, and her husband obligingly built temples and shrines to accommodate them all. We can let God be the judge of his character: 'There was never a man like Ahab, who sold himself to do evil in the eyes of the Lord, urged on by Jezebel his wife. He behaved in the vilest manner by going after idols' (1 Kings 21:25–26).

As an act of judgement, God had commissioned his prophet Elijah to warn of a terrible and prolonged drought with all its bitter consequences. Elijah delivered the warning and was sent away by God to hide east of the river Jordan, at a secluded spot where ravens brought him bread and meat each day. This was not to keep Elijah safe, but to deny the people access to the prophet. Disobedience always removes access to God; which, of course, was the very point of the Lord's reminder in Nazareth if only the leaders had a mind to understand. He was saying in effect, if you reject me, the good news of the kingdom will bypass you and go to the Gentiles, just as in the time of Elijah.

As the drought took hold, the little brook that supplied Elijah ran dry. God could so easily have opened an underground stream to keep the waters flowing—or for that matter, the ravens could have added bottled water to the daily provisions! But instead, God sent the prophet on a long journey 'to Zarephath of Sidon' and ordered him to stay there (1 Kings 17:9). God did not have to send him there; Elijah was perfectly safe where he was and God could easily have supplied all his needs.

So why did God remove Elijah from the seclusion of that desert hide-out to the pagan and exposed city of Sidon? The answer is simply that God had plans for a widow woman in the village of Zarephath close by Sidon. God knew that not all in Israel had 'bowed down to Baal' and that at least seven thousand were still loyal to the truth (1 Kings 19:18), but for all that great number in Israel, he did not overlook a poor widow far away in Zarephath who had kept herself from idols to serve the living God. If he knows when a sparrow falls to the ground (Matthew 10:29), he must surely be able to watch over this desolate woman and her child. Somewhere right in the heartland of idolatry, and far from the land of Judah in the south where godly Jehoshaphat was on the throne, lived a widow and her son. She was surrounded by a vile mixture of the fertility rituals at the Asherah, the antics of the prophets of Baal (there was a magnificent temple to him in Tyre, just down the road, which Ahab later copied in Samaria), and above all, her own national god Eshmun.

But this widow was different. Somehow, she had learnt of the Lord and she trusted him. She may have been an Israelite widowed and destitute, though it is more likely she was not from either Israel or Judah, but was a Gentile who, in this far-away land had found the true God. That would certainly fit the use Jesus made of her in Luke 4. She is here to remind us not only that God reached beyond the borders of Israel, but that he knows his people wherever they are and however isolated they may be. Surely a comfort to thousands of Christians across the world today in China, and the closed countries where Islam denies freedom, and the refugee centres struggling with the meaning of terrible earthquakes, tsunamis and tornadoes. Alone and isolated she may be, but God knows his people wherever they are, and God sent his prophet on a long and dangerous journey—just for her.

The evidence of her faith was that she somehow recognized Elijah as a prophet, perhaps because of his dress and bearing (see 2 Kings 1:8), and her reply in 1 Kings 17:12 was a confident: 'As surely as the Lord your God lives'. If ever there was an illustration of God's electing grace—choosing to show mercy on those far away—we have found it in the story of this widow. God has his people in the most unlikely places and calls them to himself. This fact was repeated in the story of the Syro-Phoenician woman so many years later. Perhaps the widow in the time of Elijah had been an idol worshipper from the very region in which Jezebel grew up—and that fact was not lost on the Jews in Nazareth; she had once bowed the knee to Baal, or Eshmun, or the Asherah—but no longer.

If there is evidence here of divine providence, there is evidence of divine humour also. Jezebel was Elijah's most vicious enemy, and here was the prophet taking refuge, and about to receive hospitality, just eight miles down the road from her home town of Sidon! This was a repeat of the experience of Moses whose death was demanded by the Pharaoh of Egypt and who ended up being clothed, fed and educated in the court and at the expense of the very man who had ordered his death: 'The Lord watches over the way of the righteous … The kings of the earth take their stand and the rulers gather together against the Lord and against his Anointed One … The One enthroned in heaven laughs; the Lord scoffs at them' (Psalm 1:6; 2:2,4). Only once did Christ teach beyond the borders of Israel, and that was close by Zarephath in the city of Sidon.

The widow's desperate need and God's decisive plan

Zarephath (the modern village of Surafend) was built on a long ridge overlooking the Mediterranean on one side and overlooked by Mount Hermon on the other. We first meet the widow just outside the city gate; she dared not venture far. Presumably there was no firewood left in the city, and she had no one to help her and her young child; the Hebrew word *ben* does not indicate the age of her son, but either he was too young to help gather firewood or too emaciated and weak with hunger. All she had was a handful of meal and a little oil, and she needed only a fire to make one last supper before they waited for the grim agony of starvation. She will have to watch her only child die, and her mother's heart was breaking. Clearly she was poor and destitute.

We all know Elijah, but although her story has been told for nearly 3,000 years, we do not even know her name: 'God chose ... the lowly things of this world and the despised things ... so that no one may boast before him' (1 Corinthians 1:27–29). It may all seem an incredible coincidence that just at the time the prophet came into town, the widow came out of the gate. Why was Elijah here? It was an out-of-the-way village in a thoroughly evil environment, and evidently the famine was no less severe here than in Israel; more than this, a prophet of Israel's God was hardly likely to find goodwill in this bastion of paganism. But, as always with God's people, there was a divine plan and procedure behind these seemingly strange events: 'Go at once to Zarephath of Sidon and stay there. I have commanded a widow in that place to supply you with food' (1 Kings 17:8).

We do not know how God commanded the widow; there is no indication that she had a dream or vision, heard voices or met with an angel. But the phrase 'I have commanded a widow' is precisely that of v 4 'I have ordered the ravens'. Whilst the word is most generally used of a command or order, it can also refer to something appointed or commissioned. The unfolding story would imply that the widow had no more premonition or knowledge than the ravens, or else she would have been prepared—which clearly she was not. We are not always aware of the way God is ordering events. The similar secret plans of God are there behind Job, Abraham, Joseph, Moses, Daniel, and all his servants in the Bible, but it is all the more encouraging to read them in the circumstances of one of the little people.

The best of faith for the widow

The first request of Elijah was reasonable—a little water could probably be spared, and she was immediately ready to share this with the man she recognized as a prophet of the Lord. But then Elijah called after her: 'And bring me, please, a piece of bread' (v 11). This was a test of her integrity and she was scrupulously honest. If she had stopped at 'I don't have any bread', the widow would have been honest to a point, but by continuing 'A little flour and oil' she laid herself open to share the final meal with a stranger and hasten her own death and that of her son.

We need not lay too much stress on her words: 'the Lord *your* God' (v 12). It was a common enough phrase in the Old Testament and did not necessarily imply that the Lord was not her God also: Joshua, Samuel and Ezra each used this phrase to Israel, and the godly prophet Obadiah used it to refer to Ahab's god.

But now a greater test came. Elijah asked to be served first! That may sound very hard. In the story of the woman and her daughter from this same area, eight hundred and seventy years later, the test was similar but the need was reversed. In that story, she is the one who wants help from Jesus and his reply: 'Why should I help you, you don't take the children's food and toss it to the dogs', was intended to draw out her moving reply that would reveal a deep-seated faith: 'Yes Lord, but dogs can have the leftovers, can't they?' Jesus commented that he had not met such faith in all Israel. That same faith is exhibited here also.

However, here in Zarephath Elijah's request was coupled with a promise that involved the name of the Lord: 'Don't be afraid. Go home and do as you have said. But first make a small cake of bread for me from what you have and bring it to me, and then make something for yourself and your son. For this is what the Lord, the God of Israel, says: "The jar of flour will not be used up and the jug of oil will not run dry until the day the Lord gives rain on the land"' (1 Kings 17:13–14).

As the widow made and baked her few cakes and brought the bread to Elijah—passing her young child whimpering with hunger—there was no evidence that the promise would be kept. She used up all her flour and oil and shared it; that was an act of faith in Elijah being a man of truth and in God keeping his promise. She stepped out in faith and saw God take care of her future: 'In keeping with the word of the Lord spoken by Elijah' (v 16). It would have been all too easy for her to suggest that she and her son should eat first and then, if he really was a prophet from God, the Lord would supply the needs of his servant. Instead, 'She did as Elijah had told her' (v 15).

There is a lesson here on not hoarding, but giving generously. Like the handful of bread and fish of the young lad involved in the feeding of the crowd on the hillside, and the widow casting a small coin into the collection box in the temple, if our little is our all, then in the hands of the master it will be commended, used and multiplied. We should not be giving God just what we can spare—our widow at Zarephath could spare nothing. Yet she offered that one meal, and she and her family were sustained for two years. Each day the meal and oil were on the point of exhaustion—and perhaps her faith was too—but with bread enough for each day, she neither fell into despair nor rose to presumption. The measure she gave was the measure she received.

The best outcome of faith is that it is always rewarded.

When Paul urged the Corinthian Christians to give as they had earlier promised, he held out to them the example of the Macedonians who: 'Out of the most severe trial, their overflowing joy and their extreme poverty welled up in rich generosity … They gave as much as they were able, and even beyond their ability. Entirely on their own, they urgently pleaded with us for the privilege of sharing in this service to the saints. And they did not do as we expected, but they gave themselves first to the Lord and then to us in keeping with God's will (2 Corinthians 8:2–5).

Had it been possible for her to know the words of Agur the son of Jaker, the widow of Zarephath would certainly have echoed the same sentiments:

Give me neither poverty nor riches, but give me only my daily bread. Otherwise, I may have too much and disown you and say, 'Who is the Lord?' Or I may become poor and steal, and so dishonour the name of my God (Proverbs 30:8–9).

And equally she would be able to agree with David:

I was young and now I am old, yet I have never seen the righteous forsaken or their children begging bread. They are always generous and lend freely; their children will be blessed (Psalm 37:25–26).

The widow's generous giving was richly reimbursed because God always pays well for hospitality given to his people—it is called a 'prophet's reward' (Matthew 10:41). A rugged prophet clothed in animals' hair and with a leather belt, became for her an 'angel without knowing' (Hebrews 13:2). But nothing has changed over the years; it is the same with our giving—whether our tithes and offerings, our time and strength or our home and prayers. None of us can have less to give in one way or another than this widow, but we are robbing God if we do not give as he expects from us. However, if we do give as we should, like her, we can stand back and watch what he will do. Her flour and oil multiplied as she used it—not as she stored it.

The widow had good reasons to deny Elijah a share in her food: she had so little, and a starving child to care for. Besides, the prophet was a stranger to her and a foreigner; what had she, a poor widow in Zarephath, to do with a prophet from Israel? But the benefit was that the prophet Elijah came and ate with her. Ours is a greater privilege, for the Lord himself has promised to come and enjoy special fellowship with those who hear his voice and obey (Revelation 3:20).

She had put the words of the prophet above her feeling and reasoning. F B Meyer, a Baptist preacher in the nineteenth century, told of a little girl who, when asked her age replied: 'I'm seven. I don't feel like seven; I feel like six, but Mother says I'm seven.' She had placed her mother's authority above her feelings and reasoning. This widow surely did not feel like sharing her remaining food, and she had some very good reasons not to, but 'She went away and did as Elijah had told her'. As a result she certainly enjoyed the experience of Psalm 37:18–19; 'The days of the blameless are known to the Lord, and their inheritance will endure for ever. In times of disaster they will not wither; in days of famine they will enjoy plenty.'

Doubtless the widow had been praying, but she never expected such a generous response. The Lord is full of surprises for those he has chosen and who are faithful to him: 'To everyone who has, more will be given' (Luke 19:26), but she did not yet know what we know, that 'Your Father knows what you need before you ask him' (Matthew 6:8).

There is another reason for this story. It is here to provide an illustration of the wideness of God's mercy then as now. Israel and Judah were slow to learn. They should have been a light for the Gentile nations (Deuteronomy 4:5–8; Isaiah 51:4–5), but they were too busy squabbling and warring among themselves to care for that. Years later Paul would write: 'Is God the God of Jews only? Is he not the God of Gentiles too?' (Romans 3:29). Significantly, Paul was repeating this nine hundred years after the story of Elijah and the widow, but the Jews were still land-locked in their thinking.

William Carey confronted an uncaring narrow-mindedness among the Northampton Baptists when, on Tuesday 29 May 1792, he preached desperately that they would set up a society to reach the world with the good news of Jesus. He was told by older heads that God could save the lost without his help if God chose to. That was perfectly correct. In fact, if he had chosen to, God could have fed Elijah without the help of this widow and the widow without the help of Elijah. But God had chosen to use a widow and her handful of meal; just as he chooses us to reach the lost—or give him whatever he is commanding us to give.

Disaster after blessing

There is a second part to this story which is as important as the first. It took place 'some time later' (1 Kings 17:17), but still in the time of the drought, because after the drought Elijah moved away (18:1). God had used a miracle to save the life of the widow's boy, and now he became so sick that he died. Why did God keep him safe for so long and then snatch him away? What sense was there in that? From the widow's viewpoint, there was no sense at all. But our view is not ever the full view. She did not know the end of the story, any more than poor Job did in his suffering—or we do in ours.

Great trial often follows great blessing, just as great blessing sometimes follows great suffering. Peter wrote: 'Dear friends, do not be surprised at the painful trial you are suffering, as though something strange were happening to you' (1 Peter 4:12). Paul wrote: 'Our present sufferings are not worth comparing with the glory that will be revealed in us' (Romans 8:18) But it hardly appears like that at the time.

Not surprisingly the widow demanded to know why her son had died. She blamed Elijah as the representative of God. She had been so calm in the face of inevitable death from hunger, but this new situation was sudden and unexpected and it caught her out. Suddenly, she forgot the daily blessings in the face of her disaster. Her immediate conclusion was that God was against her. It must be punishment for the past. That is an age-old half-truth. In one sense it is always true, since all suffering here is the result of the entrance of sin into the world. Sometimes it is wholly true: it took the death of their father to bring to the forefront of the minds of Jacob's sons the terrible crime of selling their brother into slavery (Genesis 50:15)—they had hoped that the passing of time would assist their amnesia.

However, tragedy is not always the result of personal sin, and those who are assured of salvation need never fear this. The disciples asked the same question of the man born blind (John 9:2): it must surely be either his fault or that of his parents. But they were to learn that it was neither; there was a purpose behind his suffering that they could not imagine: it was that the glory of God might be displayed (v 3). That is always the purpose behind suffering—whether the breakdown of our health or of our plans—if only we could see it this way with the eye of faith. Besides, in a world of suffering, those who trust God cannot expect to be immune from affliction: 'Shall we accept good from God, and not trouble?' was Job's wise and realistic conclusion (Job 2:10).

From her accusation: 'Did you come to remind me of my sin?' the widow's mind may have returned to something she had long tried to forget—perhaps the years she had spent involved in pagan fertility rituals. It is often the case that personal tragedy reminds us of personal sin. She felt like Job: 'You write down bitter things against me and make me inherit the sins of my youth' (Job 13:26). But that is never God's way with those whom he has forgiven. When he forgives, he promises never to recall those sins that are covered over: 'I ... am he who blots out your transgressions, for my own sake, and remembers your sins no more' (Isaiah 43:25), and more specifically: 'Do not be afraid; you will not suffer shame. Do not fear disgrace; you will not be humiliated. You will forget the shame of your youth and remember no more the reproach of your widowhood' (54:4).

So, why this tragedy? Perhaps the widow was resting too comfortably in the unfailing provision of God. Day by day, whilst the world around starved, she enjoyed the supply of food that was found in her box of meal and jar of oil, and she had come to take it for granted. That strikes very close to the mark for those of us living in the comfort and plenty of a western lifestyle. Or perhaps she had grown a little proud of the fact that the prophet had come to *her*. Just as life was continuing so securely, God shook her and humbled her.

Here was the widow, holding close to her heart her last consolation which had been so suddenly snatched away from her. Where was Elijah when the child grew 'worse and worse' (v 17)? But God is never in a hurry, and the same happened with the death of Lazarus; Jesus delayed for two days until his friend was dead.

At the end of the story we take leave of the widow with the words 'Now I know' on her lips (v 24). But did not the meal and oil convince her of the truth? After daily miracles for months, her faith failed at one more test. Perhaps, all the time she could fight to keep her child alive there was a determination to press on; during the long months of the famine the widow had a reason to stay alive and hope. But now that her child was dead, all her faith and hope fled from her and she forgot the Lord's provision in the past. Like her, we receive provision daily from the Lord and experience his kindness days without number; then something goes 'wrong' and our carefully laid plans fall apart—and God is to blame.

If the widow heard the first prayer of Elijah, it would have been altogether discouraging. He was not the most optimistic of men at any time: 'O Lord my God, have you brought tragedy also upon this widow I am staying with, by causing her son to die?' (v 20). 'Tragedy' was precisely how she viewed it, and if the prophet could rise no higher than that, she was left without hope. Like the story of Job, *we* can see the big picture behind it all, and *we* may wonder at the seeming lack of confidence in God from Elijah at this moment. But the story is here to alert us to the fact that there is always a big picture behind every event in our own lives. Seeing the invisible is the life of faith that God calls all his people to live.

The child was brought back to life. And what was the significance of that? There is no story of a resurrection before this one. Elijah had no example to rely on, nothing to bolster his faith—and neither had she.

What is more, the very first miracle of bringing back to life from the dead recorded in the Bible, took place outside Israel and in the territory of Eshmun the god of healing and health!

In that one act, God judged a faithless nation and mocked an unbelieving nation. Before long, the prophet would take on Baal the god of storm, and defeat him on a calm day on Mount Carmel. Meanwhile, the widow of Zarephath leaves the pages of the Bible with at least a word of confidence on her lips: 'Now I know'. The word of the Lord is always truth, whatever our circumstances; his purposes, often blindingly concealed, will come to fruition in his time and not ours. If she learnt much from her experience with the meal and oil, and the death of her child, we learn so much more from her response.

Naaman's servant—a little witness goes a long way

'If only my master would see the prophet who is in Samaria! He would cure him of his leprosy' (2 Kings 5:3)

Ben-Hadad, the king of Aram, had desperately needed a few good victories for his army. In recent memory, he had suffered two humiliating defeats by Ahab, king of Israel. Ben-Hadad had mustered the entire army and threatened Ahab who was holed up in his capital at Samaria. In response to a promise from the Lord, Israel had been given an unexpected and overwhelming victory and Ben-Hadad barely escaped with his life. However, Ben-Hadad returned to the attack the following spring with a new and larger army (1 Kings 20). For seven days the two camps faced each other, but whilst the army of Israel looked like two small flocks of goats, the hosts of Aram seemed to cover the entire countryside. However, this time Ben-Hadad was forced to surrender and throw himself on the mercy of Ahab. Foolishly, the king of Israel simply extracted reparations from him and released him, on the basis that Ben-Hadad was 'my brother' (v 32).

That claim had more than a little historical truth behind it, since the Aramaeans were descended from the line of Shem, who was one of the sons of Noah (Genesis 10:21–23), and both Isaac and Jacob had Aramaean wives. For two centuries prior to King Saul, the tribes of Aram had been flowing into Syria and Mesopotamia until they became a powerful force and a constant threat to Israel. They gradually merged with the Syrians and that is why some translations of 2 Kings 5:1 refer to the king as 'king of Syria', though the Hebrew word here is *Aram*. Saul later fought vigorously against the Aramaeans, though David married an Aramaean princess and their son Absalom was the unhappy result.

After that rash treaty with Ben-Hadad, there had been peace for three years during which time Ben-Hadad was yet again building an army to challenge Israel. There is some dispute among scholars as to whether, in the account of the king of Aram, we have one king with a long reign or father and son with two shorter reigns, but what we do know for certain is that it was Naaman who had given the king of Aram his long-awaited triumph over Ahab: 'Naaman was commander of the army of the king of Aram. He was a great man in the sight of his master and highly regarded, because through him the lord had given victory to Aram. He was a valiant soldier …' (2 Kings 5:1).

Now the tables had been turned. Jewish tradition has it that it was Naaman himself who 'drew his bow at random and hit the king of Israel between the sections of his armour' (1 Kings 22:34). Whether or not this is true, Ahab died of his wounds and was buried in Samaria and Ahaziah his son succeeded him in the year 853 BC. But his reign was brief, and two years later Jehoram (sometimes spelt Joram) came to the throne of Israel. He is the king of Israel in the story of the Hebrew maid which opens in 2 Kings 5.

Naaman was a powerful man in the Aramaean nation and probably second only to the king himself. Success in battle carried with it honours and respect, riches and influence. But for all this, there was one terrible blight on the family of this famed military general: he had leprosy. The exact nature of his illness is not known and it may not have been the leprosy that we are familiar with today. In the culture of Israel, all severe cases of skin disease necessitated that the sufferer was isolated from the community in order to prevent the spread of an infection (Leviticus 13:46). That something similar was the custom in Syria is implied by the statement of the servant girl: 'If only my master would see the prophet who is in Samaria! He would *cure* him of his leprosy' (2 Kings 5:4). The word *acaph* that she used is repeated in the king's letter (v 6), and it is a reference to being restored or gathered back into society; it is not the normal word for healing, which is *rapha*. As an illustration of this, the word *acaph* is used in Numbers 12:14 of Miriam being 'brought back' into the community after her own punishment of leprosy. Therefore the servant girl wanted her master to be restored to the family and to normal life in society; this, of course, implied healing, but it was a healing in every realm that she doubtless prayed for.

This great commander had a death sentence written in his body and he was no longer able to command the king's forces. He was avoided by those who once respected him and perhaps he felt as Job had when he contracted a terrible skin disease and found himself alone outside the city and despised by his friends and even by his own wife:

My kinsmen have gone away; my friends have forgotten me. My guests and my maidservants count me a stranger; they look upon me as an alien. I summon my servant, but he does not answer, though I beg him with my own mouth. My breath is offensive to my wife; I am loathsome to my own brothers. Even the little boys scorn me; when I appear, they ridicule me. All my intimate friends detest me; those I love have turned against me. I am nothing but skin and bones; I have escaped by only the skin of my teeth (Job 19:14–20).

A terrible gloom had settled on the household because, unlike Job, there was no hope or comfort for Naaman, either in this life or beyond the grave. Job had gone on to reaffirm his confidence in God in that magnificent statement:

I know that my Redeemer lives, and that in the end he will stand upon the earth. And after my skin has been destroyed, yet in my flesh I will see God; I myself will see him with my own eyes—I, and not another. How my heart yearns within me! (Job 19:25–27).

Naaman's god, Rimmon, offered no such help or hope. It was all night in the household of this once proud warrior, and everyone walked in silence, misery and fear. The master was no longer at home and his wife and family cried constantly. But there was just one small star shining in the darkness.

The servant girl's faith

The young servant girl was the only one in the household of Naaman who knew for certain what her ultimate future was; like Job, she knew her Redeemer and she wanted to share her good news with her master. As with so many of God's little people in the Bible, there is much more to the narrative of the young Hebrew servant than is at first obvious. That long military struggle between Israel and Aram is significant to her story. Even during the uneasy peace between the two kingdoms, and certainly throughout the preparations for hostilities, raiding parties from both sides would frequently penetrate the frontiers of the enemy; this is alluded to in the truce that subsequently followed the humiliating defeat under Naaman's command when 'the bands from Aram stopped raiding Israel's territory' (2 Kings 6:23). These raiding parties were designed to probe and test the position, strength and determination of the enemy, but they also provided a steady flow of booty, which included captives for the slave market.

It was on just such a raid that the servant girl was snatched from her family and carried into the home of the commander of the army of Aram.

The words that describe her are brief but specific. She was only a girl and she was young; the word 'young' can also mean small or insignificant, and all of these words would fit. We do not know her name, her home town, her family or her future. We can only hope that she was treated well as a result of what happened to her master; perhaps she was set free, though that may not have been possible since if her parents had been killed or sold, she had no home to return to.

The little maid had grown up in Israel at a time when the religious life of the nation was at a low ebb. None of the kings of the northern part of the country were spiritual men, and the legacy of wicked Ahab and his even more malicious wife, Jezebel, was still felt in the time of Jehoram. Only the courageous work of the prophets of God kept spiritual life alive. Clearly this young girl had been brought up to trust the teaching of the prophets, and her parents were among the godly of the land—but even that did not prevent the family being torn apart by the raiding bands of Naaman. Trust in God does not guarantee that the tragic circumstances of life will never touch the Christian, but it does promise a useful life and an ultimate hope, as her story shows.

The maid knew her God was in control, even though there was little evidence of this around her. The phrase referring to Naaman 'through him the LORD had given victory' (v 1) would have surely been how the servant girl viewed it also. Her understanding of God was such that not only was the military success of this pagan commander under the control of her

God, but doubtless that is how she understood her own heart-wrenching tragedy of being torn away from her family. Such a strong theology was what enabled her to be calm and compassionate in a strange land and among a people who were her nation's enemies. She believed that, 'There is no wisdom, no insight, no plan that can succeed against the lord. The horse is made ready for the day of battle, but victory rests with the Lord' (Proverbs 21:30–31).

Like Joseph in the court of Egypt and Esther in the palace of Persia, this insignificant servant girl, though snatched from the security of a loving family and dragged into a hostile land, believed that she was here with a purpose and that her God, unlike the local pagan deities, would not forsake her but would come with her into exile. Her God was not confined to Israel. Long before the mighty Naaman came to understand it, she knew that the Lord was God, the only God, of the whole world. Small, young and insignificant she may be, but she was a giant in faith and theology. She knew what mattered in Israel. All that she had been taught about Elisha she did not forget. What had she seen him do? Or what had she heard about him? Perhaps very little. But what she knew, she believed.

In her mind, there was no possibility of failure: if only Naaman could just *see* Elisha, he would be restored to his family and friends once again (v 3). How could she be so sure? She had never seen anyone healed of leprosy, and she had never heard of anyone being restored from such a disease. According to Luke 4:27 there were 'many' in Israel with leprosy and not one had been healed. Apart from this, there are only a few recorded miracles from Elisha's ministry, and even if we assume many more, it may be questioned how many she would have known about. Here was a faith that expressed confidence beyond her understanding. This young girl lived with a faith beyond her sight (see 2 Corinthians 5:7).

If only we had the same confidence in our God to believe that, though we do not see him at work as we would love to, yet he is the unchanged and unchanging God of power and authority.

All around her was the hopelessness of false religion. Swept from a land where few trusted the true God into a land where none did; she was alone with her faith. Even Daniel had more friends with him in Babylon than she had in Aram. She was a true Daniela in Syria. Her master's god was called

Rimmon (v 18). He was the storm god Hadad, which meant 'Thunderer', and his symbol was a bolt of lightning and a thunder club. Thus the name of the king, Ben-Hadad, meant 'son of Hadad' the storm god. Across the whole of the ancient Near East, though more usually under the name Baal, he was the most important deity of all; locally his temple was in Damascus.

The servant girl's faithfulness

One outstanding question in the whole of her story is why Naaman believed her? After all, she was only a servant girl and had been stolen from the enemy; she had no reason to wish for the welfare of her master. It is evident that Naaman was a proud man, as his response to Elisha's order to bathe in the Jordan reveals, and this is the reason why Elisha refused to pander to his conceit and come out to him with due reverence and perform some magic by incantations (vs 11–12). So why on earth should the commander in chief of the Syrian army take notice of, least of all heed the advice of, his own foreign servant—and an insignificant girl at that! We may wonder if he eventually slipped away to Samaria without her knowledge so that he would be less humiliated if it all proved to be a false hope.

It is very possible that Naaman had heard of the prophet Elisha and even his predecessor, Elijah; that contest between Elijah and the prophets of Baal in the time of Ahab had left four hundred pagan priests dead, and the story must have gone the rounds of the local tribes. But there is surely more to his trust in her story than this. Had the family already seen something different about her? She was not sullen or resentful, on the contrary she was a willing and honest servant. This Daniela was clearly a personal servant to the commander's wife. The word translated 'served' in v 2 is more specific than that. It is made up from the word for a face and implies that she served as a personal maid. Many servants in the Georgian and Victorian English country mansions would never be seen on the stairs after early morning lest they meet 'the lady of the house'; so not all servants in the ancient world came into the presence of their mistress, they simply carried out orders. However, the trusted servants would become personal assistants. The same word is used in the following verse when she longed that her master would 'see' Elisha. The word is literally 'the face of' and refers to the immediate presence of someone. Significantly it is used in Exodus 33:14 when God promised Moses 'my Presence (literally 'my face') will go with you.' In days before our clear silvered mirrors, the only way that anyone could see someone's face was to be in their immediate presence. This servant girl was a trusted personal maid to Naaman's wife.

Throughout her personal tragedy, she remained true to her faith. She lived out what she believed and allowed the laws of the God of Israel to govern her life. This Daniela did not harbour revenge. Hers was a heart of compassion for the man who had stolen her from her family. The phrase '*If only* my master would see the prophet who is in Samaria' (v 2) well brings out the expression she used which is more like 'Oh that!'. She obviously felt for the family's distress at this time, even though we might have forgiven her for taking a very different attitude: 'Serves them right; now they know how *I* feel.' On the contrary, her only concern was the welfare of her master. That must have made a huge impression on her mistress. True 'Christian' compassion always does. Long before our Lord underlined it, this maid knew the meaning of 'love your enemies, bless those who curse you, do good to those who hate you, and pray for those who spitefully use you' (Matthew 5:44). If we harbour a grudge, bitterness, resentment or anger against someone, we would do well to learn from this young servant girl.

God was reaching out to the nations. According to Luke 4:27, 'There were many in Israel with leprosy in the time of Elisha the prophet, yet not one of them was cleansed—only Naaman the Syrian.' This was unusual in the Old Testament but not unique. Rahab the Canaanite, Ruth the Moabite, Ashur-dan III the Assyrian and the widow of Zarephath the Phoenician—all these were reached by Joshua, Naomi, Jonah and Elijah. But now God used a seemingly unimportant servant girl. Here is the gospel in the Old Testament. This is the great commission in action centuries before it was given by Christ to his church. She was ready to be used and therefore God used her.

The servant girl's fearlessness

This little Daniela was prepared to take a great risk. It was a ridiculous suggestion that her master could be healed from his leprosy—in living memory no such miracle had ever occurred either in Israel or in the land of the Aramaeans. We may not be sure exactly what the disease was, but according to Jesus, there were many with the same complaint and he was the only one cured.. But what if he had not been cured? What if Naaman had taken that journey to Israel, and Elisha had refused to see him, or had disappeared? Or the prophet was simply unable to help? If Naaman had come back unhealed but humiliated—woe betide this servant girl! She was vulnerable in the extreme. So are we all when we tell the truth about the Saviour. That is what so often puts us off witnessing: the fear of things not going right. What will people think, or say or do?

Without intending, and without knowing, she almost started an international crisis. When Jehoram received the official request from Ben-Hadad, he assumed that the old enemy of Israel was simply looking for an excuse for a new outbreak of hostilities (2 Kings 5:7). But for the timely intervention of Elisha, war would have commenced yet again—and it would have been all *her* fault. Given the dire possibilities if her master had not been healed, it took immense courage even to make her suggestion— but faith like hers is always courageous. It was not the amount of faith that counted, but where she placed her confidence.

The story of Naaman's healing is well known, and need not delay us. But how sincere was his 'conversion'? His claim 'Now I know that there is no God in all the world except in Israel … your servant will never again make burnt offerings and sacrifices to any other god but the Lord' (v 15,17) was clearly not intended as a passing concession to the God of Israel. In fact, it was a massive claim for a worshipper of local gods. When Naaman had sought the help of what he considered to be the local deity of Israel, this was no violation of his cult worship in Syria; unlike the Jews who were soundly condemned for having anything to do with the false gods of the nations, there were few, if any, false gods for Naaman or his king, only different localized deities. Few religions at that time believed in one God of the 'whole world'. Each nation, even locality, worshipped gods and goddesses who belonged to a territory (like the mountain or valley), or elements (like the storm, sun or moon), and they were happily prepared to adopt others into their pantheon. But the idea of a universal God who excluded all others was largely unknown to them.

When Rameses II of Egypt made a peace treaty with the Hittite king, Hattusilis, it was the gods of both nations that were called to witness: 'As for him who shall keep these terms written on this silver tablet, the thousand gods of Hatti and the thousand gods of Egypt will cause him to flourish and will make him live, together with his household, his lands and his servants.' Similarly, Cyrus, the Persian king who defeated the Babylonians and allowed the Jews and other nations to return to their own lands and rebuild the temples to their gods (see 2 Chronicles 36:23), saw this as no violation of his worship of 'Marduk the great god' and boasted: 'The gods whose abode is in the midst of them, I returned to their places and housed them in lasting abodes.' He acknowledged that in bringing these gods into Babylon, Nabonidus, the last Babylonian king, had offended 'Marduk, the great lord', but he did not deny their right to 'dwell in peace' back in their own lands.

The fact that Naaman wanted to take back soil from Israel reflected that, understandably, he was still thinking as a pagan: he could only worship a national god on its own territory. But at least he was determined to take this God seriously and for this reason he asked of Elisha only forgiveness if he had to attend the local religious ceremonies of Rimmon with his master; a request incidentally that Elisha wisely ignored. How truly converted to the God of Israel he was is impossible for us to know for certain, except that the phrase 'no God in all the world except in Israel' was a massive shift in the mindset of a worshipper right across the lands of the ancient world.

All the evidence at the time, and the fact that our Lord used him as an illustration of God reaching across in grace with the gospel to the nations (Luke 4:27), points in a positive direction. But for us, the more important fact is to see how and through whom God reached out. In the light of her story, is there anyone whom God cannot or will not use for the spread of his kingdom? All he required of this servant girl was a willing obedience and a humble submission to his plans.

Mary King was the school cook when Charles Haddon Spurgeon attended the Newmarket Academy, but to her the Victorian Baptist pastor, who has been called 'the Prince of Preachers', attributed his grasp of theology; he supported her in later life. Maria Millis was nanny to Lord Shaftesbury, the Seventh Earl and great philanthropist who became 'Lord of the great unwashed'. As a boy he dreaded his boarding school yet hated to return home where his parents cared for nothing but politics and high society; yet to Maria Millis he said he owed his spiritual life as she taught him about the Saviour. On her death, she left her watch to him and he wore it ever after. Elizabeth Newton died before her only son reached his seventh birthday, but not before she had stored his mind with the Bible and the hymns of Isaac Watts, and prayed that he might enter the Christian ministry. Elizabeth did not live to see her son become a blasphemous, debauched and godless seaman, but neither did she live to hear of his miraculous conversion in an Atlantic storm and of the future vital gospel ministry of John Newton as an Anglican clergyman. A little witness goes a long way.

Whether or not Naaman's servant was rewarded for her kindness we cannot know. At least we can be certain that she was thrilled when she enquired as to the meaning of the two donkey loads of soil that were dumped in the backyard on his return (v 17). Was she allowed to worship Yahweh with him? Did he ask her advice on how best to worship the only God of the world? What was her relationship with her mistress from here on? Did she remain as a servant? Was she offered her freedom? We can only speculate for the answers.

But the story becomes even more intriguing.

That experience with Elisha had a significant military value for Naaman. Some time later Ben-Hadad ordered a renewed offensive against Israel; this must have placed Naaman in a difficult position, but he was a military man and obeyed his orders. When it became apparent that every strategy planned by the king and his commanders was known to Jehoram, we may presume that it was Naaman who had no difficulty guessing where the information was coming from; he was more than likely the officer referred to in 2 Kings 6:12 who identified Elisha as the one who 'tells the king of Israel the very words you speak in your bedroom'. Despatched to the walled town of Dothan, Naaman suffered the humiliation that he and his troops were struck blind, led in a circuitous route to Samaria where, in the total control of King Jehoram they were feasted and freed instead of being butchered. That too should have made Naaman think. Yet again the young servant girl's great God had shown mercy to her master.

Whether or not the story of Naaman ended at the subsequent siege of Samaria by the Aramaean army and the final rout of the besieging forces which is told in 2 Kings 7, we cannot know. But what we do know is that the story of this young Daniela still holds a fascination for those who follow the God of the whole world and, like our Lord's beautiful promise for the faithful action of the woman who, in the house of Simon (another man healed from leprosy), poured perfume over Jesus: 'wherever this gospel is preached throughout the world, what she has done will also be told, in memory of her' (Matthew 26:13).

Martha and Mary—the priority of praise

'Wherever the gospel is preached throughout the world, what she has done will also be told, in memory of her' Mark 14:9

Jesus was a familiar guest in the home of Lazarus and his two sisters. Bethany, not to be confused with 'Bethany on the other side of the Jordan' where John the Baptist baptised (John 1:28) and whose exact location is still hotly debated by archaeologists, was just under two miles east of Jerusalem. The little village must have offered a haven of calm during the hectic ministry of Christ, and the close friendship of Lazarus, the busy attentiveness of Martha, and the deep devotion of Mary all fitted into a beautiful theme that provided a home of warm and welcome hospitality. There are six women called Mary in the New Testament, but since there is little danger of confusing Mary of Bethany with any of the others, we need not unravel them all; her name was as popular in Palestine as Martha's was uncommon. There is only one Martha in the New Testament, and in fact the name has so far not been found outside the New Testament in the first century. The two sisters appear on just three occasions, one of which is repeated in all the Gospels apart from Luke. In order of happening, we have the two women at home (Luke 10:38–42), by the grave of their brother (John 11:1–45), and as guests in the home of Simon the Leper (John 12:1–8, Matthew 26:6–16 and Mark 14:1–10).

When a story is repeated three times in the four Gospels, it does not mean that it is more reliable, but it should make us stop and take notice that it is something on which God places a high priority. It is not more true than any other part of Scripture, but it may be more important than some. This is particularly so when twice we are informed that wherever the good news is preached, this episode will be told.

It is not difficult for us to piece together the story of Martha and Mary, but before we do that, we must clear away a few misunderstandings. First of all, the account of Mary anointing the feet of our Lord with an expensive perfume must not be confused with the story of a different woman recorded in Luke 7:38–50. This too was in the home of a man called Simon (v 40) though this was by far the most common name among Jews in first-century Palestine and Galilee and it is therefore most unlikely to have been 'Simon the Leper' in our story of Mary. In addition, the details and the occasion are different: Luke 7 records events in the region of Galilee and much earlier in the ministry of Jesus, and the subject of the episode was an unnamed woman who was notorious in the district for her loose living. The focus in Luke 7 is on the kind of woman she was and the scandal of her gate-crashing the party, whereas the focus in each of the three accounts of the story of Mary is on the 'waste' of such an expensive perfume. Luke was not confusing the two incidents, he knew perfectly well who Mary of Bethany was and he does not mention her in chapter 7.

Which leads us to the second possible misunderstanding: Luke is the only Gospel writer not to refer to the story of Mary of Bethany anointing the feet of Jesus, but he does tell us about a different meal—this time in the home of Mary, Martha and Lazarus—at which Mary plays a prominent part (Luke 10:38–42). We must not confuse these two meals either.

There are three stories, and each revolves significantly around Mary, and between them they reveal two aspects of her in particular: the priorities of her life, and the passion of her worship; though the character of Martha is neither unimportant nor wholly negative,

Martha and Mary at home

Luke introduces us to this family immediately after he has recounted the parable of the good Samaritan, and it is probably the one story of Mary that most are familiar with. Martha, whose name appropriately means 'lady' or 'mistress', was certainly in charge of the home. Apart from John 11:1 her name always appears first, and clearly she was the more hospitable of the two sisters. Martha was the one who had 'opened her home' to Jesus (Luke 10:38), and she was now busy preparing the meal. She may not have been one of the women who supported Christ and his disciples by travelling around with them (Luke 8:2–3), but her home was always open, and it was as much her delight as that of her sister to welcome Jesus at the family table.

Her busyness in the kitchen was vital to the welfare of Jesus and his disciples. But at times Martha lost sight of the priorities, and she doubtless thought that about Mary as well. We must not be too hard on Martha. She had at least fifteen or sixteen to cater for, since the disciples were almost certainly present, and she was all alone whilst her sister was sitting idly doing nothing. Martha was 'distracted'—pulled in all directions—and 'worried and upset'. Finally she exploded and both Mary and Jesus felt the edge of her tongue. Mary was accused of being idle, and Jesus of encouraging her. Martha was doubtless thinking: 'If she is not prepared to work, she need not bother to eat either.' That she was het up is clear from the fact that our Lord had to use her name twice to calm her down, and then rebuke her for allowing her priorities to get out of line (v 41).

However, we must not be too sympathetic with Martha either. Clearly our Lord would not have rebuked her if everything she was doing was just right. Martha was doing the right thing to an excess that spoiled it. When she complained that Mary 'has left me to do the work', there is at least an implication that Mary *had* been helping earlier; but perhaps she lost patience with Martha's finicky attention to unnecessary detail. When hospitality becomes a burdensome chore, perhaps we are trying too hard to please. Peter used a very expressive word to encourage hospitality: 'Offer hospitality to one another without grumbling' (1 Peter 4:9). When our hospitality, or whatever we do for the Lord, leads to a grumbling spirit or robs us of time to worship, then we have somewhere lost our priority.

Perhaps the story recorded in Luke 10 contrasts the two women perfectly. Mary was perhaps known as something of a dreamer; probably not very practical, and certainly not the busy, dedicated domestic like her sister. But nothing distracted Mary from focussing on her Lord—it is appropriate that the most likely meaning of Mary's name is 'beloved'.

As Jesus was talking to his disciples, Mary edged herself closer and sat on the floor at his feet, listening intently. It was not her intention to avoid helping out in the kitchen, nor did she simply enjoy a 'good sermon'. Mary wanted to hear the words of the Lord in order to do what he said. Unlike so many then and now, she had 'ears to hear' what he had to say. Later, Jesus told his disciples: 'If you love me, you will obey what I command' (John 14:15). Obedience is one of the best expressions of our love for the Lord, and certainly there can be no real devotion to Christ unless we give evidence of a sincere desire to listen carefully to what he has to say—and then to obey. Mary was not an idle listener, as is clear from our Lord's response. She had made the wiser decision for the better activity, and he would not deny her that privilege. By implication he might have added: 'Leave the meal, Martha, we'll eat it as it is; come and sit with Mary.'

Martha and Mary at the grave of their brother

When Lazarus was first taken ill, the sisters sent a message to Jesus that 'the one you love is sick'. Jesus appeared to do nothing, except delay heading for Bethany, and so Lazarus died. The moment she heard that Jesus was not far from the village, Martha got up and went straight out to meet him (John 11:20). Mary, on the other hand, sat at home until Jesus called for her. That too was so predictable of the two sisters. Is there significance in the fact that John records the fact that many of the Jews 'had come to visit Mary' (v 45)? Surely they would have come to comfort and mourn with both the sisters? Or is it likely that they knew Martha could cope more rationally at a time like this? It would be Mary who needed the greatest attention; her sensitive nature was likely to fall apart at such a time of terrible loss.

We do not need to imagine what Martha and Mary had been talking about over the past few days, because Martha's first comment to Jesus and Mary's first comment are identical. When they each separately met Jesus the first thing they blurted out was, 'Lord, if you had been here, my brother would not have died' (vs 21, 32). With tears streaming down their cheeks and with breaking hearts, they rehearsed over and over again to each other: 'Why didn't he come? If only he had been here it would have been allright. If only he had been here our brother would not have died.'

However, when Mary came to Jesus she seems to have forgotten something else they had been talking about. It was Martha who added: 'But I know that even now God will give you whatever you ask' (v 22). That was so typical of Martha: ever the practical, chatty person, she expressed her hope in clear and cogent words; Martha did not exactly tell Jesus what to do, but she certainly got her message across. Mary, on the other hand, simply blurted out their long rehearsed line and then fell at Jesus' feet in tears (vs 32–33). She had a massive problem and her response was silence. Her trust was silent.

It would be unjust and foolish to pit the response of one sister against the other at this point. We are looking at two very different characters, and each responded to their tragedy and expressed their faith in their own way. Martha could frame words, precise words, in any situation; whether she was angry or broken-hearted no one would doubt what Martha intended. Mary was very different. In Romans 8:26 Paul wrote about those occasions when we do not know how to pray or what words to use. It is at that point that the Spirit 'intercedes for us with groans that words cannot express'. Mary's groans were just tears. She fell down before the Lord, and with a breaking heart had such a trust in him that she had nothing to say. Mary's unspoken trust moved the incarnate Christ to tears more than Martha's reasoning. Perhaps, at this moment, Mary's silence was worth more than Martha's chatter.

Actually Martha betrayed herself in verse 39. When Jesus told them to roll the stone away, Martha's immediate reaction was: 'Oh no, Lord, you can't do that. He's been dead four days and there will be a terrible smell.' Our bold words of trust often evaporate when the Master puts them to the test. Peter learned this the hard way. For all his courageous intentions to die with Jesus (Matthew 26:35), he was the one who denied his Lord three times. Mary was silent because her trust was absolute. She left it with the Lord whom she knew could only do right and only act wisely, whatever he did.

Sometimes our trust is heard more in our reverent silence than in our excited chatter; more in the things we don't say, than in the things we do say; more in the inclination of the heart than the movement of the tongue; and more in the things we silently lift to heaven than the words we loudly sing from the hymn book or screen.

I shall never forget the value of the words of Bill Bygroves, the pastor of Bridge Chapel in Liverpool, at a time of great trauma in the life of my wife Barbara and myself. They came on the tape 'My times are in his hands', and we played them over and over again:

I walked a mile with pleasure, she chatted all the way.
But I was none the wiser for all she had to say.
I walked a mile with sorrow, never a word said she.
But, oh the things I learnt that day, when sorrow walked with me.

However, at the close of the story of the raising of Lazarus, it is Martha who stands out for her strong profession of faith. It was Martha who reaffirmed her confidence that her brother would rise again in the resurrection at the last day (v 24). It was Martha who responded so positively to Christ, assuring him that she not only believed that was he the 'resurrection and the life', and that 'whoever lives and believes in me will never die' (v 25), but Martha added from her own understanding: 'You are the Christ, the Son of God, who was to come into the world' (v 27). In a touching postscript, Martha ran back to fetch her sister: 'The Teacher is here, and is asking for you.'

What follows is interesting, and typical of the character of Mary. She got up quickly and went, probably ran, to Jesus. Clearly the group of mourners had not heard Martha's whisper that Jesus was asking for her, because they thought Mary would be going to the tomb (v 31). Perhaps when they saw her heading in the opposite direction they would call to her that she had gone the wrong way. But Mary ignored them, just as she had ignored her sister's lashing tongue on the previous occasion—and would ignore the painful reprimand of the men in the future. When it came to meeting with her Lord, nothing would hinder Mary.

Poor Martha, yet again, received something of a rebuke from Jesus, and rightly so. All her confidence in the ability of Christ and who he was seemed to collapse when Jesus ordered the tomb to be unsealed; the thought of the smell and the sight of the decomposing body of her brother was just too much and she objected in the commanding way she was accustomed to. Surely Jesus should know better! His response was to remind Martha of their conversation just a few minutes earlier when he had reassured her that 'Your brother will rise again.' Now he rebuked her for her forgetfulness: 'Did I not tell you that if you believed, you would see the glory of God?' (v 40). There is a tantalizing silence in Scripture over the reaction of the two sisters when their brother walked free from the tomb—but we can imagine the scene. What *is* recorded, is the fact that whilst some who had come to mourn with Mary now believed, others sneaked off to report the whole episode to the Pharisees (vs 45–46).

Martha and Mary in the home of Simon the Leper

The third story we will follow from the record of John 12, though both Matthew and Mark record it also, and they inform us that it took place in the home of 'Simon the Leper' (Matthew 26:6). It was six days before the Passover when our Lord came to Bethany and stayed at the home of Lazarus and his two sisters. Four days later, and therefore just forty-eight hours before his death, Jesus was invited to a meal in the home of Simon who had been suffering from leprosy until, presumably, Jesus healed him. Perhaps Simon and Lazarus were related, because somehow Martha found herself serving at the meal; she was that kind of woman who naturally gravitated to the kitchen. There is no shame in that, because there is no indication that on this occasion Martha was doing anything other than the right thing in the right way. Perhaps the meal was a celebration for the raising of Lazarus and the healing of Simon, and an expression of gratitude to Jesus.

However, there is an obvious contrast in John 12:2–3. Martha was busy serving as usual, whilst Mary took a jar or bottle of perfume—it is called an alabastron—snapped the sealed long neck, and poured it over the head of Jesus until it ran down his clothes; then using her long hair, she wiped the perfume to his feet. Matthew and Mark tell us that she 'poured' the perfume over Jesus, whilst John goes to the significance of the act and uses the word 'anointed'. The perfume was pure, expensive, and there was a lot of it—half a litre! The 'nard' or spikenard was expertly extracted from a plant of the valerian family and was prized for its beautiful scent. It is hardly surprising that the whole house was filled with the fragrance of it; presumably replacing the aroma of Martha's well-prepared meal!

Who else ever showed such adoring love for Christ as Mary? The disciples left their business to follow Christ, and some invited him into their home and laid on a meal for him. But no one else ever showed such adoration with the single exception of the other woman whose story is recorded in Luke 7. Why did Mary show such adoration? Not because she was especially bad, and not because she was particularly good, though it is clear that she was a woman of deep devotion whose godly reputation was well known. The reason Mary showed such devotion was that Christ was such a wonderful person, and she recognized this—and what he would later accomplish for her.

Jesus commented that what Mary did for him in the home of Simon the Leper was in preparation for his burial. It was common practice to anoint a dead body before burial with perfumes and spices in order to counter the putrefaction of the decomposing body; this would be done until there was time to provide a proper burial. For this reason the women purchased spices and went to the tomb of Jesus in the garden of Joseph of Arimathea on that morning after the crucifixion (Mark 16:1). Mary intended her action to be in preparation for his burial because she understood that he was shortly to die.

Remember, Mary was a great listener, and those who spend most time hearing the words of Christ will have the deepest understanding of the purposes of Christ. If that is the case, we must not pass over this event lightly. The men could not grasp the significance of these final days—not one of them. More than once Jesus spelt out clearly what lay ahead and still they did not understand his meaning. Peter had assured Jesus that it would not happen like that and certainly not while Peter was around. But Mary understood; because she had a heart inclined towards him, she knew who he was. And her adoration was costly. When Judas worked it out, it was a year's wages for a labourer.

A workman's annual wage! Where did Mary get that much? Doubtless she had been saving it. What for? She might have been saving it for her wedding day. But there was no greater priority in Mary's life than the worship of Christ. The highest activity in which anyone can be engaged is the adoration of the Saviour. Peter made great professions, and his theology at Caesarea Philippi was very accurate: 'You are the Christ, the son of the living God'. But at the very end of our Lord's relationship with Peter on earth he asked him three times: 'Peter, do you love me?' Jesus never asked Mary that question.

In the light of the forthcoming momentous events of the Last Supper, the betrayal, arrest, trial, crucifixion and resurrection, this may seem a rather trivial episode. Outside, the city was alive with religious zeal—this was Passover time, one of the most important religious events in the Jewish calendar. It was also a dangerous time when Jewish nationalism was stirred and emotions ran high; the Passover evoked all the memories of slavery and the hope of freedom. The Romans were particularly vigilant at this time of the year in Jerusalem, and it would be an ideal time for the Pharisees to bring Jesus of Nazareth before the Roman governor as a trouble-maker. He would be more likely to clear up the business with a quick execution as a warning to other would-be disturbers of the peace of Rome. Just two days before his trial, surely Christ should be laying out plans to keep the movement going after his death; there was little time left. And yet the story reads so casually. This was the last act of sincere homage that our Lord would receive before his crucifixion; the cruel betrayal and the mocking scorn and beating from rough soldiers was all that he could expect from now on.

Everyone was angry with Mary: a dozen or more men—and especially Judas. Her action appeared irrelevant at a time like this; unrealistic and wasteful. By contrast, the men were thoughtful and practical. Out there is a world full of the poor, that's where the money should go. Worship is all very well, but there are surely bigger priorities. Besides, this was an intrusion into the meal: 'Not now Mary.'

For Judas it was a matter of 'Not at all Mary.' He could see nothing more than a waste of money, time and effort. How did worship like this help the world? He who was pilfering from the common purse (John 12:6) was suddenly the greatest philanthropist in town. Our Lord's response to Mary seems to have been the final straw for Judas, because Mark notes that immediately at the close of this episode: 'Then Judas Iscariot, one of the Twelve, went to the chief priests to betray Jesus to them' (Mark 14:10).

Mary received a sound lashing from the tongue of the disciples and, if I judge her sensitive character correctly, it must have reduced her to tears. She perhaps thought everyone would be pleased at her simple act of devotion, but far from it; she was accused of prodigal waste instead. The phrase 'rebuked her harshly' (Mark 14:5) is a fair translation because the word carries with it the idea of a stern reprimand. In the eyes of the world, Mary could never get it right.

For a moment our Lord allowed their anger to run its course, and Mary must have been waiting for his rebuke as well. But what she heard was something very different:

Leave her alone … Why are you bothering her? She has done a beautiful thing to me. The poor you will always have with you, and you can help them any time you want. But you will not always have me. She did what she could. She poured perfume on my body beforehand to prepare for my burial. I tell you the truth, wherever the gospel is preached throughout the world, what she has done will also be told, in memory of her (vs 6–9).

If Mary was not already in tears, she would be now!

He who had spent three years of his public ministry devoting his time and energy to the needs of the poor, the sick and the possessed, hardly needed a lesson from his disciples on priorities. The poor are important but, contrary to the typical view of the world, the worship of Christ is far more important. And the reason for this is that in falling humbly before Jesus and acknowledging the value of his life, death and resurrection, we reveal the true state of our heart in caring for others. The words of Judas and the action of Mary are all that is needed to prove this point.

Mary is a challenge to those who are so busy with life that they have little time to sit and listen to the voice of Jesus in his word; she is also a challenge to all who are so easily distracted from the opportunity of worship, whether private—in what used to be called 'the quiet time'—or with the congregation of the Lord's people. It is our attitude to worship that betrays our hearts. The world says it is a waste of time; we could be doing much more useful and productive things. The taunts of friends and family, even our hobbies, sport, or good works, can entice us away from worship. Mary experienced all that, but her devotion was undeviating.

What Jesus thought of Mary

Perhaps the key to these three stories of Martha and Mary is found in our Lord's commentary in the home of Simon: 'The poor you will always have with you, and you can help them any time you want. But you will not always have me' (Mark 14:7). There is a time and place for everything. Martha was preoccupied with administration, whilst the disciples focused on poor relief—both were good causes and excellent tasks. In their place and on the right occasion they are essential, as Paul in Romans 12:7–8 made clear. However, the focus on this occasion should have been on Jesus. In the home of Simon, only Mary understood this: 'she has done this for my burial.'

Worship is a priority when it should be a priority.

An all-exclusive busyness is not a substitute for adoration and praise. To rush into the day by omitting time with the Lord is never justified—even when the busyness belongs to his work. Certainly all that we do should be done in the name of Jesus and for the glory of God (Colossians 3:17), but that must never be in the place of time to be still and look and listen to God. Daily, we should find time to 'lean on the windowsill of heaven and gaze upon our God.'

Most have a sneaking sympathy for Martha, and most of us can readily identify with her. But let the Lord be the judge between us as we survey his comments on Mary's actions.

'Mary has chosen what is better' (Luke 10:42). Her 'better' was a listening ear to the voice of Jesus, and a commitment to worship and adoration of the Saviour she loved.

'It is the one thing necessary', Jesus assured her, and added 'it will not be taken away from her.' Nothing matters more than to be obedient to the word of the Lord.

'Leave her alone' Jesus commanded, '… it was intended that she should save this perfume for the day of my burial' (John 12:7). That was his protective response to the adoration of Mary in the home of Simon.

One philosopher wrote, 'Human beings have the choice of adoration or annihilation.' He was wrong, because there is no such thing as annihilation. We live for ever either with or without adoration. Jesus added, 'She has done a beautiful thing to me' (Mark 14:6). How valuable if our worship, alone and when we come among God's people, is a beautiful thing to God. Her worship was very personal, undoubtedly costly and certainly Christ-centred—that is why it was beautiful.

When the Lord commented that, 'She did what she could' (Mark 14:8) I think he meant, 'she has done the best that she was able to.' But that was typical of Mary: only the best would do for her Lord. Perhaps Mary was just not cut out for the culinary skills of the kitchen, and her sensitive character would never place her in the front line of aggressive evangelism; perhaps she did not have faith to remove mountains and would never be big in the eyes of the world—she would always be one of God's little people. But Mary could worship Christ for his death and resurrection, and allow that to speak volumes to those who would take notice.

Jesus added, 'Wherever the gospel is preached throughout the world, what she has done will also be told, in memory of her' (Mark 14:9). There was something wonderfully evangelistic about Mary's worship; if the house 'was filled with the fragrance of the perfume' (John 12:3), that was only a small picture of the real extent of her action. Two thousand years later, her story is still being told across the world. True worship from lives and hearts that are wholly committed to Christ will always be a powerful evangelistic tool. Paul longed that unbelievers would sense the presence of God in the congregational worship of the believers at Corinth (1 Corinthians 14:25)—and that should be true whenever God's people worship together.

There are only two occasions where we read of Jesus weeping. As he came towards Jerusalem with the crowds shouting their praises and the leaders snarling their opposition, Jesus saw in his mind the terrible devastation that would come upon the city within the lifetime of the children around him, and he wept out his sadness: 'If you, even you, had only known on this day what would bring you peace—but now it is hidden from your eyes' (Luke 19:41). He wept over darkened minds and unbelieving hearts. The only other occasion when Jesus wept was when he saw the sadness around the tomb of his friend Lazarus, and especially the tears of Mary; it is here that we have the shortest verse in the Bible: 'Jesus wept' (John 11:35). Mary's simple trust, her unbroken faith and her tears, reduced the Son of God on earth to tears. Therefore, only two things recorded in the Gospels brought tears to the eyes of Jesus Christ: The hardness of unrepentant hearts, and the quiet adoration and trustful tears of Mary.

If Christ were here on earth, what, in my life, would bring tears to his eyes?

Mary was a woman of sincere actions but very few words. In the Gospel stories she sat listening to Christ, anointed Jesus with an expensive perfume, and wept at the grave of her brother. But each story brings her to the feet of Jesus: In the home she 'sat at his feet', in the house of Simon she 'anointed his feet', and at the grave of her brother 'Mary fell at his feet'. Mary knew just where true worship begins. But she said very little. For all the chatter of her sister, the only recorded words of Mary are in John 11:32, and they are just ten in the Greek: 'Lord, if you had been here, my brother would not have died.' Worship is not all noise and activity. It is a Christ centred heart, a Christ-occupied mind, and a Christ-filled soul.

Mary Magdalene—messenger of the resurrection

'Mary Magdalene went to the disciples with the news: "I have seen the Lord"' John 20:18

Of all the women in the Bible, it is Mary Magdalene who has stolen the media headlines in recent years. In 2003 a book reached no. 1 on the *New York Times* best-seller list, and it stayed there for thirty-five weeks. The book was *The Da Vinci Code*, and its author was Dan Brown. On 3 November 2003 fifteen million Americans heard his testimony on the breakfast programme *Good Morning America,* in which he claimed that his book was not only a novel, but much of it was scholarly fact—real history. But what has this to do with Mary of Magdala who is one of six Marys in the New Testament and who is mentioned on just six occasions?

Back in the second century, shortly after the four Gospels—Matthew, Mark, Luke and John—had been generally accepted among the churches as the definitive story of the life, death and resurrection of Christ, the leaders of the churches began writing against a form of heresy that was circulating, known as Gnosticism. In brief, the title 'Gnostics' comes from the Greek word for knowledge and refers to the secret mysteries that they believed were not available to all. The Gnostics believed in two gods—the incorruptible God revealed in the New Testament and the demiurge, an evil god revealed through the Old Testament; the real Jesus, who was not God, was substituted on the cross by an ordinary man and thus salvation is not a sin-bearing atonement but grasping a knowledge of the mysteries.

For nearly two thousand years almost all we knew of this strange pseudo-Christian philosophy was what the early church leaders told us in their defence of the orthodox faith. Then, in 1945, out in the deserts of Egypt, a shepherd discovered by accident a collection of ancient books hidden in the sand. These books are now known as the Nag Hammadi Library and they reveal that what the early church leaders told us about Gnosticism was an accurate description of what the sect believed, because the Nag Hammadi Library, which was first published in English in 1977, is a collection of Gnostic books. It lists forty-five titles including five that claim to be 'gospels', all written in the second or third centuries AD: the Gospels of Truth, of Thomas, of Philip, of the Egyptians and the Gospel of Mary. And that is where our Mary of Magdala comes into the story.

Under the pretence of scholarship, Dan Brown set out in his book, *The Da Vinci Code*, to show that the real story of Jesus was recorded in these Gnostic writings, and that the fourth-century church set out to systematically destroy these records and put in their place what we know as the four Gospels. The novel claims that 'Constantine (the first Roman Emperor to embrace Christianity) commissioned and financed a new Bible, which omitted those gospels that spoke of human traits and embellished those gospels that made him godlike. The early gospels were outlawed, gathered up and burned' (p.234). So, everything taught about Jesus since the fourth century is false! In reality, these Gnostic gospels supposedly contain the vital information that Jesus was actually married to Mary Magdalene, had children by him, and that his blood-line continued in Europe. But where does the title of the book: *The Da Vinci Code* come in? It is Dan Brown's contention that when the famous fifteenth-century Italian artist Leonardo Da Vinci painted his picture *The Last Supper*, he knew all about this relationship of Jesus with Mary of Magdalene and that the figure to the right of our Lord at the table, generally supposed to be the apostle John, is in reality none other that Mary herself. *That*, is the Da Vinci code.

It is not difficult to debunk the so called 'scholarship' of Dan Brown. Long before the fourth century, all the books of the New Testament were in wide circulation; a list, known today as the Muratorian Canon, is dated around AD 150 and, among the New Testament books, it names only the four Gospels that we are familiar with. In the same century a church leader, Irenaeus, refers to the four Gospels alone and, in a clear attack on the Gnostics, condemns those who distinguish between Jesus the man and the Christ who is divine. There is plenty more evidence that long before the time of Constantine in the fourth century, our New Testament books, as we know them, were all accepted by the church as authoritative—and no more. In fact, the most obvious reason why the writings of the Gnostics were lost for almost 2,000 years, was not because they were destroyed by the church in the third century, but because the Gnostics died out and their writings with them.

But what of the story of the relationship between Jesus and Mary? Not even that dusty Egyptian library of Gnostic books claims that they were married; there is not one statement making such a claim.

There is one other piece of fiction that we must dispense with, though this is not claimed by *The Da Vinci Code*. It is assumed by many that before her contact with Christ, Mary had been a prostitute. This is a confusion with the unnamed immoral woman, whose beautiful story is recorded in Luke 7:36–50, who gatecrashed a dinner party and wiped the feet of Jesus with her tears, her hair and a large quantity of expensive perfume. This story was never linked with Mary of Magdalene until Pope Gregory the Great confused the two in a devotional sermon in AD 591.

Mary in service

Mary was a popular first-century name and therefore it is to be expected that some form of identification was needed to distinguish her in the Gospels from Mary the mother of Jesus, Mary the mother of James and Mary the sister of Martha. If she had no relatives who would be known to the followers of Jesus, then to designate her by her birthplace would be quite normal. Magdala was a wealthy city on the western shores of Galilee, some three miles south of Capernaum. Its affluence is measured by the fact that the tribute it sent to Jerusalem had to be conveyed in wagons! Yet, for all its wealth—perhaps because of it—Magdala was known to be a dissolute city of extravagance and immorality. This is another reason why some have considered Mary to have been a prostitute, but that is unwarranted speculation.

What we do know, however, is that Christ had cast out seven demons from her life (Luke 8:2). We must not follow the line of some superficial commentators in assuming that the Gospel writers attributed all illnesses to 'demon possession'. Matthew and Luke are especially careful to distinguish between various diseases, severe pain, the demon-possessed, the epileptics and the paralytics (see Matthew 4:24 *English Standard Version*), and they do not attribute demon-possession to all who are mentally afflicted in one way or another.

Demon-possession is clearly seen when a life is taken over by foreign spirits who plague the whole being with their evil intentions. During the life and ministry of Jesus, there appears to have been an upsurge of demonic influence throughout Galilee and Palestine, and this is hardly surprising since the reason the Son of God had come was to 'destroy the devil's work' (1 John 3:8).

Exactly how this terrible affliction shattered Mary's life or how she came to be so battered by Satanic forces, and when she first met the Saviour who immediately released her from her slavery, none of this we are told. What we do know, however, is that she soon found herself in company with a number of other women who had similar experiences of Christ's power to release them from 'evil spirits and diseases'. Their gratitude drew them to him and to one another, and they determined to assist his ministry in the only way they could.

The fact that some of these women came from a wealthy and influential background is evident from the reference to 'Joanna the wife of Chuza, the manager of Herod's household' (Luke 8:3). This was Herod Antipas who, on the death of his father, Herod the Great, became tetrarch of Galilee and Perea (Luke 3:1); he committed adultery with his half-brother's wife Herodias, was condemned by John the Baptist and ordered John's execution. Luke is the only Gospel writer to refer to Joanna, and she may well have been his informant for the later events in the palace of Herod recorded in chapter 23:6–12. Chuza held an important and responsible post in the royal palace, and his wife would have had the personal means to support Jesus and his disciples both with money and food.

There would be nothing unusual about women in the first century having sufficient property to 'support them out of their own means'. During the years of Christ's childhood, a woman called Eumachia in Pompeii controlled a brick-making company and provided a temple for the headquarters of the wool traders and fullers; she dedicated it to the emperor Augustus and his wife Livia and was a priestess there; it was a richly adorned building of marble. Similarly, in AD 43, shortly before Paul's first visit to Corinth, Junia Theodora, a wealthy woman in that city, was extravagantly commended by the citizens for her hospitality and her generosity. She was encouraged to 'increase her generosity to our city', and for their part the citizens 'will not cease in their good will and gratitude to her, and will do everything for the excellence and glory she deserves.'

Luke had a special interest in mentioning the women of social status who responded to the gospel: at Thessalonica (Acts 17:4), Berea (v 12), Athens (v 34), and Philippi (16:14). It is Luke also who draws our attention to the home of Mary, the mother of John Mark where the disciples met regularly for prayer (12:12), and to Dorcas, 'who was always doing good and helping the poor' (9:36).

The word that is used of the assistance that these women gave to Jesus and his disciples in the phrase 'helping to support them' is the word for service (*diakonos*). Interestingly it is precisely this word that is used by Paul in Romans 16:1 of Phoebe's service to the churches. She may well have been a business woman who, in the course of her trade, travelled among the churches and supported the work of the gospel in every way possible; Paul himself was grateful to her for her help. When he referred to her 'great help' (v 2), the word he used was that of a female guardian or patron, caring for the affairs of others and aiding them with her resources. That was precisely the ministry of Mary Magdalene and the other women.

Our modern society, in its warped sense of priorities and a determination to downgrade the value of the Bible, not only scoffs at the idea of a woman assisting with domestic help, but assumes that this is a demeaning task for her. It clearly was not, in the eyes of Dr Luke or of the Master he served. Without the help of these women, the apostles would not have been able to devote themselves to the work of the kingdom of God; Peter, James, John, Andrew, Philip and the others would have been back on the lake fishing, or whatever their trade, and Matthew would have returned to his accountancy.

But the service of Mary Magdalene and her friends was not a passing expression of fleeting gratitude. Clearly they were travelling about with Jesus and the disciples (Luke 8:1–3); this was a costly business for them, and one wonders how Joanna managed this unless her husband, in addition to being the manager of Herod's household, was also a secret disciple. But more than this, when Jesus left Galilee and moved into Judea, many of the women followed. Matthew is insistent that Mary Magdalene was among those who 'Had followed Jesus from Galilee to care for his needs' (Matthew 27:55) and who now stood silently weeping at his cross.

What does 'caring for his needs' mean in the Christian church today? There are a thousand small, usually unsung and often overlooked, ministries in the life of a local church and the work of the gospel. Perhaps few know, and fewer commend—but the Master knows that they are done for him. Those who are 'busy at home' (Titus 2:5) are equally 'caring for his needs'. Each worker in the church has gifts to serve for the gospel (Romans 12:6–8) and just as no one should think of themselves too highly (v 3), so none should think of themselves too meanly either. Over two thousand years, the church has grown by the multiplication of small service in caring for the needs of the community.

We must never fall into the trap of the world by downsizing the significant task of a servant. We will see how Mary was rewarded very soon.

Mary at the cross

The next time we meet with Mary of Magdala, she is among the women at the cross. Luke does not mention her by name (23:49), but Matthew does: 'Many women were there, watching from a distance. They had followed Jesus from Galilee to care for his needs. Among them were Mary Magdalene, Mary the mother of James and Joses, and the mother of Zebedee's sons' (27:56). John mentions her also (19:25) and Mark (15:40). There can be no doubt that she was there. But what is particularly significant is that Mary had faithfully followed Jesus and the apostles from Galilee. We cannot be sure of the precise chronology, but certainly Mary had been with the Lord and the apostles for the better part of a year or more. Not only had she witnessed the remarkable miracles of Jesus, but she was also doubtless aware of the growing hostility towards him from the Jewish leaders. The future was overcast by the clouds of the approaching fury of the Pharisees—but that did not deter Mary.

Just where Mary was at the arrest of Jesus, we do not know, but there can be little doubt that as soon as she heard of it, she would be found moving close to the action. One thing is certain, when Jesus was roughed-up by Pilate's soldiers and hauled off to Herod, Mary's friend, Joanna, would have kept her well informed of all that was going on in the palace. As Christ was dragged through the city and out of the gate to the place called 'The Skull', we can hardly doubt that Mary was among the 'large number of people [who] followed him, including women who mourned and wailed for him' (Luke 23:27). In fact, John is explicit in informing us that at the moment of his crucifixion, some of the women, together with the disciple John, were very close to the cross—and Mary was one of them (John 19:25). They were so close that Jesus could, with his dying, labouring breath, speak to his mother and his disciple. Mary heard it all, and with streaming eyes watched the agony of the Man who had so marvellously transformed her life from a bitter bondage to evil spirits to a new freedom she had never before experienced.

Later, it would seem that the soldiers forced all onlookers to move back, because Matthew, Mark and Luke each record that the women stood 'at a distance'. It is likely that when Jesus told John to look after his mother for him, the apostle led her away from a scene that she must have found terribly distressing. From the three lists of named women in Matthew, Mark and Luke we may gather that Mary, the mother of Jesus was among them, as was her sister, who is possibly the one named Salome—the wife of Zebedee and thus the mother of James and John; Mary the wife of Clopas and the mother of James and Joses was also there, and since it is clear that there were others, we may assume that Joanna was there also. But the one referred to by all three writers is Mary from Magdala. Of the eleven apostles only one, John, is named as being present anywhere near the cross! All honour to the courage of these women, though it has to be admitted that they stood in less danger than the men, since the Romans were hardly likely to see a group of sobbing women as a threat to peace and order. If a rescue attempt came from anywhere, it would be from men.

Mary was there when they crucified her Lord; she listened in to the conversation between Jesus and the robbers, and his gentle command to John and his mother Mary; she heard his agonizing cry from the cross, stood terrified in the shuddering darkness, and marvelled at the response of the centurion: 'Surely this was a righteous man—this man was the Son of God.' But when all fell silent and the crowds drifted off, Mary stayed, along with some of the other women. Wondering what would happen next she winced as the cruel spear was thrust into the side of Jesus, watched curiously as a military messenger arrived on the scene and the centurion in charge left his men and hurried off. She did not know that he had been ordered to report to Pilate in person to confirm that all three prisoners were dead.

Mary was still there when two men arrived and began to remove the body of Jesus from his cross. Perhaps one of the women recognized them, and in the fading light whispered their identification to the others: 'It's Joseph from Arimathea and Nicodemus, both members of the Sanhedrin!' Nicodemus was carrying a large and clearly heavy box of spices—myrrh and aloes, and Joseph unfolded the linen with which they would wrap the body (John 19:38–40). As the two men gently carried the body into the gathering darkness, the women followed (Luke 23:55). They must have made themselves known to Joseph and Nicodemus because they not only entered the private garden of Joseph, but they 'saw the tomb and how his body was laid in it'. Even when the other women slowly and sadly returned home, Mary Magdalene and Mary the mother of James and Joses remained behind for a while (Matthew 27:61).

Mary on Sunday morning

Saturday—the Sabbath day—must have been a nightmare! Jewish regulations forbade them from anointing a dead body on this day, and it must have been long hours of unrelieved gloom for all the disciples. Locked in the home of Mary, John Mark's mother, the men were fearful that the Jews or Romans would round up all the followers of Jesus. For their part the women, between their sobbing and comforting one another, were preparing more spices to anoint the body of their Lord.

Perhaps they had asked permission of Joseph to return to his garden, but if so he would probably have advised them not to bother: he had heard that the Sanhedrin warned Pilate that there was a real possibility that the disciples of Jesus would attempt to steal his body and declare that he had risen from the dead, then 'This last deception will be worse than the first'

(Matthew 27:64). So, with a Roman guard at the entrance to the garden, and the Governor's personal seal on the tomb, no one would be allowed near the place.

According to Mark, as soon as the Sabbath was over—that would be after 6 pm on the Saturday—Mary Magdalene went with two of her friends to buy spices in the market place (Mark 16:1). The market must have been buzzing with talk of the crucifixions and scary darkness of the previous day.

It was very early on Sunday morning when the women ventured into the garden; it was still dark, though the sun was just casting its warm glow above the Kidron Valley. But by the time they arrived at the tomb, they could see their way more clearly. Mary Magdalene with Mary, the mother of James, and Salome came 'to look at the tomb', but also with spices 'to anoint Jesus' body' (Matthew 28:1; Mark 16:1). Oblivious to imperial guards and seals, they were drawn as by a magnet to the place where the Lord's body lay. Apparently the 'violent earthquake' and the rolling back of the stone by an angel had already taken place before Mary and her friends entered the garden, and what is equally clear is that the guards were too petrified to intervene when the women approached the tomb.

On the way they had been discussing how they could roll the stone away from the tomb, but when they arrived, on either side of the entrance sat two angels, one of whom spoke gently to the women:

Why do you look for the living among the dead? Don't be afraid, for I know that you are looking for Jesus of Nazareth, who was crucified. He is not here; he has risen, just as he said. Remember how he told you, while he was still with you in Galilee: 'The Son of Man must be delivered into the hands of sinful men, be crucified and on the third day be raised again.' Come and see the place where he lay. Then go quickly and tell his disciples and Peter: 'He has risen from the dead and is going ahead of you into Galilee. There you will see him, just as he told you' (Matthew 28:5–7; Mark 16:6–7; Luke 24:5–7).

Assuring each other that the tomb really was empty, they came out into the breaking dawn, and the comment by Mark that they were 'trembling and bewildered' (v 8) must be something of an understatement!

At this point we follow the story of Mary in the record of John 20:1–18.

Mustering all her failing courage she broke away from the others and returned to the tomb to reassure herself that the stone really had been rolled back. Mary wheeled round to rush to the disciples, somehow passing in the gloom the other women following on behind. Blurting out her story to Peter and John: 'They have taken the Lord out of the tomb and we don't know where they have put him,' she returned with the two sceptical disciples who nevertheless felt it was worth investigating. By now the guards had left their post to report the strange and frightening events to the chief priests (Matthew 28:11–15). John outran Peter, but when he arrived, Peter rushed into the tomb, 'saw and believed'(John 20:8). When they hurried back, not immediately to the other disciples, but to their lodgings (v 10), Mary was left once more alone in the still quiet of the garden.

Plucking up her courage again, Mary peered into the tomb and saw two angels sitting where the body of Jesus had lain. Gently they asked her, 'Woman, why are you crying?' and through her pitiable sobs Mary pleaded, 'They have taken my Lord away, and I don't know where they have put him.'

Then followed the most beautiful story of all the resurrection appearances.

Perhaps Mary heard a movement behind her, or just sensed the presence of someone. Whatever made her turn round, Mary came face to face with her risen Lord. But her blinding tears twisted everything into a dim outline and in a moment of inconsolable distress, she thought she was talking to Joseph's private gardener! 'Woman,' the figure enquired, 'why are you crying? Who is it you are looking for?' Mary's pathetic response is for ever to her credit; 'Sir, if you have carried him away, tell me where you have put him, and I will get him.' There was a rugged determination in Mary, that wherever, and by whoever, the body of her Lord had been stolen away, she, Mary Magdalene, out of whom he had cast seven demons and whose life he had radically changed, would go and get him—though it may cost her her life. That was the depth of her determined devotion to Christ.

It took just one more word from Jesus to transform the whole scene: 'Mariam' is the word he actually used. This was her true Aramaic name that she had been given by her parents, and Jesus now used this affectionate and familiar term that she would recognize at once. Mary had heard him use it scores of times as she sat listening to his teaching or busied herself in serving the disciples. There was no mistaking his voice. Mary turned towards him and cried out in Aramaic, 'Rabboni!'—literally 'my teacher'.

At this point we may imagine that Mary fell at his feet and grasped his ankles because his response 'Do not hold on to me, for I have not yet returned to the Father', was not intended as an unkind rebuttal of her affection, but to help Mary appreciate that from now on, none of his disciples would enjoy the same kind of fellowship with him that they had become accustomed to over the past three years; they must get used to enjoying a spiritual rather than a physical relationship—by faith and not sight. He would be with them, but in the spirit and not in the flesh.

Writing in the third century, one of the early church leaders, Hippolytus, refers to Mary as 'an apostle to the apostles'. Some have made too much of this, because all that Hippolytus meant was that Mary was given the inestimable privilege of being the first to carry to the disciples the good news of the resurrection of Christ. Mary Magdalene was the first to see the risen Christ and the first to declare this glorious fact to the world. Her orders were simple and yet profound: 'Go … to my brothers and tell them, "I am returning to my Father and your Father, to my God and your God."'

Inevitably Mary was obedient to the command, she went to the disciples with the news: 'I have seen the Lord!' and she eagerly told them all that he had said to her. But the disciples had little confidence in the testimony of one woman, because John records that by the evening the disciples were still locked in fear of the Jews (20:19). Besides, Mark informs us that when Mary reported her meeting to the disciples, they simply 'did not believe it' (Mark 16:11). Peter and John were apparently not present to confirm their part of the story.

This must have been the most shattering experience of her life. The arrest, trial and crucifixion of her Lord were bad enough, but when Mary finally met with the risen Lord, heard him speak to her, touched him herself, and was convinced that he was alive and then returned with the excited and glorious news that Jesus was risen from the dead—no one believed her. Perhaps, after all, she had imagined it; perhaps they were right when they comforted her with the consolation that they understood her distress and wishful imagination. It takes courage to hold to your experience of Christ as a risen and personal Saviour when a cynical world mocks at your faith.

Meanwhile, with an excited and near hysteric mingling of fear and joy the other women had already fled from the tomb and may have been out of the garden—when they almost bumped into Jesus! They must have recognized him, because they fell at his feet and worshipped. Repeating the encouragement of the angels earlier, the Lord told them: 'Do not be afraid. Go and tell my brothers to go to Galilee; there they will see me' (Matthew 28:10). This seems to have been one instruction they were surprisingly unwilling to obey because in their fear, their immediate reaction was to say 'nothing to anyone' (Mark 16:8). When eventually they did pluck up the courage to share their news with the disciples, their worst fears were realized: the disciples 'did not believe the women, because their words seemed to them like nonsense' (Luke 24:11).

The story of how the disciples were finally convinced is not our concern here. What matters is the magnificent historic fact that when Jesus, the eternal Son of God, rose from the dead—the most incredible and powerful event in all history—he chose first to appear not to Peter, or his three inner-circle disciples, but to Mary, out of whom he had cast seven demons. And when he gave the first instruction to go and tell the triumphant message of the resurrection, he gave it to Mary, who had so devotedly served him and ministered to his needs in Galilee and Judea.

Is it any wonder that Satan should try to smear the reputation of such a privileged woman by making up stories about her and her relationship with Jesus?

Mary stands as a supreme message of the value of God's little women. If we were to take one character from the Gospel records, and award that person the privilege of meeting first with the risen Jesus, who would it be? Perhaps Peter, who for all his miserable failure, loved his Lord passionately. Or Joseph of Arimathea, who was emboldened by the cross to declare openly his commitment to Christ by providing a tomb for his decent burial. Or Lazarus, whom Jesus loved so much that his early death caused the Saviour to weep. Or even Mary his own mother whose heart bore the piercing of a sword as she suffered, as any mother would, with all that her Son suffered. Or the apostle John, the disciple whom Jesus loved. But not

Mary of Magdalene—who did little more than provide his food and care for his needs, who simply, in her own simple way, 'ministered to him'. But that is precisely who Jesus chose for such a privilege. Remember his word to you: 'I tell you the truth, whatever you did for one of the least of these brothers of mine, you did for me' (Matthew 25:40).

When we serve one another, in however small a way, we serve Christ. Our privilege also, like Mary's, is to witness to his resurrection. We do not see him as she did, but our faith is as real, our assurance as strong, and our joy as great. To Thomas, Jesus promised 'Blessed are those who have not seen and yet have believed' (John 20:29).

Lydia—an open heart for the truth

'The Lord opened her heart to respond to Paul's message' Acts 16:14

Some of those who were converted in the early sweep of the gospel across Greece and Asia were among the wealthy and elite in the empire. Crispus, the synagogue ruler at Corinth (Acts 18:8 and 1 Corinthians 1:14), was certainly one of these since he would have been chosen partly because of his ability to assist in the upkeep of the synagogue. Titius Justus, a near neighbour of Crispus, was at least sufficiently wealthy to own his own home (Acts 18:7). Similarly, Stephanas in the same city was a householder who was able to devote himself 'to the service of the saints' (1 Corinthians 16:15). However, men were not the only privileged class, because many women in the first century ran successful businesses and reached prominence in society; some of these are referred to in Acts, though not by name, as 'God fearing women of high standing' and 'prominent' women (13:50;17:4,12). The word translated 'prominent' carries the meaning of influential and wealthy.

We saw in the previous chapter on Mary Magdalene that this was not untypical during the first century. Eumachia at Pompeii and Junia Theodora at Corinth were both wealthy women and prominent citizens in their community. In the interesting 'Polytarch inscription', a second-century dedication from Thessalonica now lodged in the British Museum, two of the men forming the town council in that Greek city are identified by the name of their mother rather than their father; an indication of the prominence of the women. One of these is 'Sosipater of Cleopatra'—though not the Cleopatra we are more familiar with.

The city of Philippi, where Lydia now lived and traded, was named after the father of Alexander the Great when Philip captured it from the

Thracians almost four hundred years before Paul arrived there. It came under the jurisdiction of Rome in 168 BC, and later Octavian (known to us as Augustus), after his defeat of Antony and Cleopatra, settled it with Italians and gave it the prestige of being considered a Roman city; to be a citizen of Philippi was to be a citizen of Rome, and the city was proud of its status. Paul's stern objection to the city officials violating the Roman citizenship of Paul and Silas would not be lost on them (Acts 16:37–39). Straddling the main highway running from Greece to Asia, Philippi was a busy city of commerce, with traders moving in and out freely.

Even by the colourful standards of Paul, his visit to Philippi was one of the most exciting episodes in the course of his mission. It was a night-time vision that brought him there in the first place (Acts 16:9), and the conversion of a poor slave girl, abused by her owners for her occult perception, led to a riot, the imprisonment of Paul and Silas, an earthquake that destroyed the local lock-up, and the salvation of the jailer and his family. But in the midst of all this was the quiet conversion of a business woman named Lydia.

Lydia and the designer trade

Clearly Lydia was not a transient merchant. She owned property in the city, and her house was sufficiently large to form the meeting place for the recently converted Jews and Gentiles (Acts 16:40). Whether she was an agent or traded on her own account we cannot know. The fact that no husband is mentioned is likely to be evidence that she was either widowed or divorced. Studies of the census returns for Roman Egypt at this time—and it is unlikely that things would have been much different in the Roman province of Asia—reveal that where home ownership can be determined, more than half of the homes were owned by a woman with no spouse; and the main causes for that were that the wife owned the chief place of residence, or the husband had died, or she was divorced—the last being the most common.

It was one of two forms of purple cloth that Lydia would have been trading in. The highest quality purple dye was derived from the shellfish of the *mollusca* family found near Tyre. The throat of each mollusc provided just one drop of the dye and thus it was a very expensive luxury and soon became an imperial monopoly. The colour was nearer scarlet than our purple. In his Gospel, John refers to the robe that was mockingly put on Christ as *porphura*—'purple' (19:2), whereas Matthew calls the robe *kokkinos*—'scarlet' (27:28). Both words were used of this coloured cloth (see Revelation 17:4 below), and Matthew and John are referring to the colour rather than the quality. Before the Romans arrived, around 190 BC, the Phoenicians controlled the market for the dye, and Thyatira was renowned for its colourful clothing which became the symbol of royalty and wealth (Revelation 18:12). However, a cheaper imitation was produced from the root of the madder herb, or the dried and crushed scale insect (the *coccidae* family), and was more generally available; it is known in modern times as 'Turkey red'. According to Acts 16:14 Lydia was trading with *porphura* which may imply the more expensive dye.

Pliny the younger, the Roman Governor of Bithynia late in the first century, wrote of 'The frantic passion for purple' across the Empire. It became a symbol of decadence, hence Revelation 17:4 'the woman was dressed in purple and scarlet'—here perhaps both the expensive and the cheaper dye are referred to. According to Pliny, 'Serious minded Romans of the Republic' would not wear it. Lydia may well have been a freedwoman working in the imperial household, in which case she traded with the highest quality dyed cloth, making a very good income as a result. Either way, Lydia was in the designer market.

Generally it was men who traded in the purple clothing, and there is at least one example of a 'purple-seller' who became a town councillor. A memorial at Thessalonica was erected in the second century by 'purple-dyers' to their colleague from Thyatira. Lydia's occupation was involved in trading with the purple cloth, rather than the dye itself, which, as we have seen, was an expensive luxury. She was clearly a successful business woman and she was certainly comfortably settled, though how prominent in the governing affairs of the city we do not know.

Lydia's birthplace lay some two hundred and fifty miles south-east of Philippi in the Roman province of Asia, now Turkey. Thyatira was a leading city in the district of Lydia which has led some to conclude that 'a woman named Lydia' is better translated 'a Lydian woman'. However, the fact that the Roman poet Horace, writing little more than half a century earlier, often used it as a proper name, means that there is no good reason to doubt that this was her true name. Thyatira was a Roman garrison city and it straddled a main trade route, ensuring its economic success. It was an important centre for the manufacture and dyeing of woollen garments, and textiles were its main source of wealth.

One thing is certain: as in medieval England, it was almost impossible to continue in any trade without becoming a member of one of the trade guilds—more trade guilds are known to have existed in Thyatira than in any other Asian city of the time. And just as the English guilds were bound up with the religious ceremonies of the Roman Catholic church, so the first-century guilds were wedded to pagan worship, often of a very immoral nature.

In Thyatira the gods Apollo and Artemis (brother and sister from Zeus) were a focus of worship, but Hermes (half brother of Apollo) was venerated as the god of commerce (cf Acts 14:12). In addition, the cult of Cybele, whose worship was well known to be sensuous, was also very popular; their music—'the soft Lydian airs'—was voluptuous.

The clash with the new religion of Christ was to present a major dilemma to the future of the Christian community in the city. When John the apostle wrote to the church at Thyatira (Revelation 2:18–25), a self-styled prophetess—'that woman Jezebel'—was leading many astray by enticing them back to the old worship of idols linked with the trade guilds (v 20). This meant 'eating of food sacrificed to idols'—and worse! Doubtless many Christians defended their action on the ground that it was not possible to make a living unless one belonged to a trade guild, and they could salve their consciences somehow. Neither John nor Lydia could tolerate such compromise; Lydia had obviously separated herself from these associations even before she became a Christian; who knows but that her bold action may have led to her husband divorcing her?

God's preparation for her salvation

Paul and his fellow missionaries, which consisted of at least Silas and Luke, met Lydia among a group of women who gathered 'outside the city gate' and close by the river Gangites. They expected to find some Jews at prayer there (Acts 16:13) since the waterside, because of its association with ritual washing, was a common place for the Jews to meet for worship, and this would naturally be outside the city walls. In fact, Jews later came to refer to those who had embraced the Jewish faith from paganism as 'a proselyte of the gate'. Though there was a small colony of Jews in Philippi, they had no synagogue of their own and Juvenal, a Roman satirist and poet who was born in AD 60, lamented that: 'The groves and streams which once were sacred ground are now let out to Jews.'

The word used to describe Lydia is drawn from the simple verb to worship, and the phrase 'a worshipper of God' (*sebomenay ton theon*) was generally reserved for those who had converted to the Jewish faith from paganism and now attended the synagogue, yet who were not committed to observe all the details of Jewish law. For the Jews themselves, a single word 'God-worshipper' (*theosebeia*) was becoming vogue at this time, and Paul once adopted that word to refer to women in the church who professed to worship God (1 Timothy 2:10). It is very likely that Lydia had come to embrace the faith of her Hebrew neighbours whilst she was living in Thyatira where there was a sizeable Jewish community. In some cities, as many as ten percent of the population were Jews, often by forced resettlement.

Clearly, Lydia was a serious and thoughtful woman who, for all her business acumen and her worldly wealth, had not allowed this to destroy her openness to the truth. She had been attracted away from her native paganism to the high morality and pure monotheistic religion of the Jewish community in her home town of Thyatira. Already she had drawn apart from the pagan guilds and yet still remained successful in business. It is always a remarkable fact when God is at work in the life of those who nudge towards the truth even whilst remaining in spiritual darkness. Lydia had not yet heard the gospel of salvation by faith in Christ through grace alone, but with as much knowledge of the true God as it was possible for her to enjoy up to this point, she worshipped Yahweh of the Hebrews. Certainly she had taken upon herself the obligation of the fourth Commandment, and on the Sabbath Lydia put aside her business and went to prayer.

Luke is careful to add that 'we sat down and began to speak' (v 13); this was a more conversational approach than a formal declaration, and Lydia was obviously prepared for the instruction of Paul and his companions.

The Lord opened her mind to understand, her heart to trust, and she responded to the message. The word implies a very close attention to what Paul was saying. Lydia knew sufficient from the Hebrew Scriptures to be prepared for a message that would lead her to the Messiah. She was certainly in the right place at the right time. This business woman became the first convert to Christ in Europe through Paul's preaching. Was she the only one converted on that occasion? We are not told specifically, though the implication is that none of the others were inclined to accept the message at this time. Just one woman—but a church was born.

The evidence of Lydia's salvation

There is a simple progression of Lydia's interest in the gospel that Luke is careful to record: 'One of those listening' (Acts 16:14) is a common expression to hear something without any particular attention; it can mean no more than a casual and passing interest, if any. But then 'The Lord opened her heart to respond to Paul's message'. The word 'opened' is not the ordinary word used to open a door, but a reference to something done thoroughly. It is used of the firstborn male child opening the womb (Luke 2:23), of the total healing of the deaf (Mark 7:34 where the Aramaic *ephratha* is reinforced by Mark with the use of the Greek word 'be opened'), and of opening the understanding to the truth (as in Acts 17:3). It is true that our part is to reason, just as Paul was doing here at the water's edge, and as he later insisted to the Corinthians: 'We demolish arguments and every pretension that sets itself up against the knowledge of God, and we take captive every thought to make it obedient to Christ' (2 Corinthians 10:5), but only the Lord can make those who are spiritually blind and deaf, seriously attentive to the message of hope in Christ.

So, Lydia was prepared as a proselyte to Judaism and that was the first step of God's grace to draw her to himself. She is a fine example of the law leading towards Christ (Galatians 3:24). Then Lydia heard the good news of Christ and the Lord opened her understanding more fully; she paid careful attention to what she heard. Finally Lydia responded to the message. We are not told exactly what Paul's message was on this occasion, but clearly he would have applied all the prophecies of the coming Messiah to Christ and declared, without hesitation, that Jesus of Nazareth was the

Son of God, by whose death and resurrection alone there is the hope of eternal salvation.

Lydia's first response was not to ask for baptism but to ask for salvation. Paul's message was never that first a person should be baptized, but that first they should be saved. The first response must be to Christ. That was always central to Paul's message: 'Jesus Christ and him crucified' (1 Corinthians 2:2) and to his purpose: 'leading the Gentiles to obey God (Romans 15:18). Paul always called for a personal response to Christ and he presented Christ, not as the solution to her marital or business problems, but to her relationship with God.

Following this vital step of faith, her next concern *was* to be baptized (v 15). This is frequently the first mark of true conversion in the Acts of the Apostles and it was intended as a public confession of her faith in Christ. Such an open profession may have been costly, but it would not have been hard for Lydia as she had already taken the bold stand to move away from her pagan roots to the faith of Israel. There is no need to read anything for or against infant baptism in the phrase 'she and the members of her household'; that subject is settled from more solid reasons than a verse like this. It would be more likely than not that these were adult members, possibly servants rather than family, who heard and responded to the same message, but we cannot be certain.

Immediately, Lydia's home was open for the gospel. It was not just a meal that Paul and his party were invited to (compare the jailer in v 34), they were encouraged to take up residence all the time they were in the city. The word that is translated 'persuaded' (v 15) is a strong expression implying compulsion by force, or in this case, by a pressing invitation. It does not mean that Paul and his company were reluctant, because they were probably lodging in a local inn up to this point, but that Lydia was insistent. The value of open home hospitality is stressed again and again in the New Testament, not only by the exhortations of Paul and Peter, but by the examples of Matthew, Zacchaeus, Mary and Martha, Mary the mother of John Mark, Priscilla and Aquila, and Gaius.

This liberality of Lydia was contagious. Some years later Paul was still grateful for their generous partnership as the Philippians shared with him liberally (Philippians 1:4–5; 4:10,15–16), and he held them up to the

Corinthians as a model of giving (2 Corinthians 8:1–5). If Lydia was the first recorded convert to Christianity in Europe, her generosity was the first example of missionary giving, and her home was also the nucleus of the first church in Europe. That her home became the central meeting place for the infant church in the city is evident from the fact that when Paul and Silas were eventually released from prison they made their way at once to Lydia's house 'where they met with the brothers and encouraged them' (Acts 16:40).

There was a simple humility about Lydia. 'If you consider me a believer' expresses her hesitancy with her new faith and she clearly wondered if Paul would consider her a Christian so soon after hearing the message. Lydia was successful in business, but she acknowledged that she was a mere infant in Christ. That is something we should never forget. The evangelical world is too often overeager to propel celebrity converts, whether from the world of entertainment, commerce or politics, into the limelight—often with disastrous results.

There is no mention of Lydia in Paul's letter to the Philippians, which is perhaps not surprising since Paul refers to very few of the 'saints' by name in that letter. However, the silence has inevitably given rise to a range of speculation about her: everything from identifying her with either Euodia or Syntyche (Philippians 4:2) to becoming Paul's wife! It is far wiser to head for the most likely explanation, which is that ten years had passed before Paul wrote his letter to the church at Philippi and it is possible that either Lydia had died in that time or had moved back to Thyatira.

What is more significant and less conjectural, is that Lydia was providing hospitality for Paul and his friends all through their turbulent stay at Philippi—apart from the brief sojourn of Paul and Silas in the local jail. Knowing her warm and caring hospitality, it is certainly tempting to wonder if she took in the slave girl after her more noisy and public conversion had led, presumably, to her being thrown out by her masters.

Lydia presents us with a beautiful character, and her gentle conversion contrasts with that of the jailer! The two had almost certainly never met before, and nothing but the gospel of Christ could ever have brought him under her roof! In her case, God quietly inclined her heart to himself, but the jailer was a far harder nut to crack, and it needed his prison to fall down around him before he would wake up to his hopeless condition without Christ. So different from one another, but now both one in Christ. We can leave the veil of silence over their future with an imaginary picture of the jailer and his family sharing in the Christian communion and love feast in the home of Lydia and her household.

Lois and Eunice—the faith of a grandmother and mother

'I have been reminded of your sincere faith, which first lived in your grandmother Lois and in your mother Eunice and, I am persuaded, now lives in you also' 2 Timothy 1:5

The church in the New Testament is too young to give us the complete life stories of its characters. Timothy is closer than any to being an exception to this, since there are many references from his childhood up to the point that we take leave of him in 2 Timothy—the final letter of Paul on record. He was born in Lystra, a remote town in Asia Minor and in the provincial region of Lycaonia; on today's map that places it a long way inland from the south coast of Turkey. In 6 BC, the emperor Augustus established a Roman colony there as a frontier post against the wild tribes of northern Galatia, but in addition to these Roman immigrants there were a number of Greeks resident in the town, including Timothy's father, and of course the local Lycaonians. Apparently and surprisingly, there was no synagogue here, even though there was a significant population of Jews.

Three languages were spoken: Latin (the official language for military and civil affairs), Greek (the common trade language) and the local Lycaonian language (Acts 14:11). In addition, the Jews would use Hebrew in reading their Scriptures. For all its isolation, Lystra was a centre for education and culture.

It was also very religious. An ancient legend, passed on by the Latin poet Ovid some fifty years earlier, tells of Zeus and Hermes (the Romans called them Jupiter and Mercury) who had come to town in the guise of humans. No hospitality had been offered to them apart from an elderly and poor couple called Philemon and his wife Baucis. The gods were angry at the selfishness of the population, and they destroyed all who had refused hospitality. For the hospitable couple however, their cottage was transformed into a temple of gold and marble, and they became its priest and priestess. We can therefore readily appreciate that when Paul and Barnabas arrived and were used by God in healing a lame man, the priest of the temple of Zeus did not want a repeat of the legend, so he made them very welcome!

Inscriptions and statues have been found in the area reflecting this worship of the gods in Lystra, including the names of two priests of Zeus, a statue dedicated to Hermes, a gift of a sun-dial to 'Zeus, the sun god', and a stone altar dedicated to 'The Hearer of Prayer, and Hermes'. Zeus was worshipped widely across this whole region and this was very likely the religion of Timothy's father.

Paul and Barnabas arrived here during their first missionary journey when they had been driven from Iconium by the Jews. A lame man was healed and Paul and Barnabas were mistaken for Zeus and Hermes. Shortly afterwards, Jews arrived from Iconium, stirred up trouble, and Paul was stoned and left for dead (Acts 14). Timothy possibly became a Christian at this time, because Paul later refers to him as: 'My true son in the faith' (1 Timothy 1:2), and 'My dear son' (2 Timothy 1:2). According to 2 Timothy 3:11, Timothy knew all about Paul's suffering at Lystra, so perhaps he was one of the disciples who helped Paul after he had been stoned and left for dead.

A reasonable guess would place Timothy in his early teens when Paul first came to Lystra and led him to Christ. The significance of this we will see later, but we can estimate his age in this way: Paul had first visited Lystra in AD 47; there is no mention of Timothy on that occasion, but it is certain that he was converted then because five years later, when Paul revisited the churches established on his first mission across Asia, Timothy is singled out for special mention: '[Paul] came to Derbe and then to Lystra, where a disciple named Timothy lived' (Acts 16:1). Since Paul had led him to Christ, it is reasonable to assume this happened on the first visit to Lystra, and now Timothy was showing sufficient signs of growth that he could be taken on mission with them (Acts 16:3). Timothy would still be considered a young man if he was in his late twenties and that would place him in his early teens before he was converted. In AD 64, seventeen years later, when Paul was writing to Timothy from his prison cell in Rome, the apostle encouraged him not to be intimidated by those who would dismiss him because of his youth (1 Timothy 4:12)—though by now he was in his early thirties!

So much for Timothy. But it is his mother and grandmother that we are especially interested in—grandmother Lois and mother Eunice. Acts 16:1–2 introduces his mother to us, and the translation is literally: 'The son of a Jewish woman believer. *But* a Greek father.' Clearly a contrast is intended, and the fact that Timothy had not been circumcised (Acts 16:3)—as he would have been if his father was a convert to Judaism—is a strong indication that Timothy's father was an unbelieving Greek. We know nothing for certain about him beyond the fact that he was a Greek. However, he was probably a well-placed local official and did not want his son to be too closely identified with the Jewish race; and this was an added reason why he did not want Timothy circumcised. Some think Timothy's father was no longer alive by Acts 16 (or by 2 Timothy), but there is no evidence either way. John Calvin thought that even Lois and Eunice were deceased by the time Paul wrote 2 Timothy; this is likely but not certain— nor does it really matter. Origen, a church leader in the third century, thought that they were relatives of Paul—but that doesn't matter either.

Lois and Eunice were women of faith

What particularly matters is that Acts 16:1 and 2 Timothy 1:5 make clear Lois and Eunice were believers. But believers in what or who? Was their faith the faith of Israel or the faith of Jesus Christ? Clearly it began as the faith of Israel, but Paul would hardly be so encouraging and commending about their faith if it had progressed no further. Besides, the word he used to refer to Eunice as a 'believing' woman is the usual way in the New Testament of describing those with true faith in Jesus Christ. No parent can expect to bring their children into personal faith if they have none themselves.

Broad Stand on Scafell Pike in the Lake District is a steep rock face, so tempting for rock climbers. Below it is a plaque that recalls the day when a father and his two sons climbing there and roped together, slipped and dragged each other to their deaths. That is a tragic parable of millions of parents today. Humanly speaking, left to his father, Timothy would never have been prepared for the preaching of Paul. Too many fathers are like Timothy's father—they would drag their children down with their own false belief, careless belief or unbelief. Some of the most threatening words of Jesus ever recorded are concerned with this very issue: 'Whoever welcomes a little child like this in my name welcomes me. But if anyone causes one of these little ones who believes in me to sin, it would be better for him to have a large millstone hung around his neck and to be drowned in the depths of the sea' (Matthew 18:5–6). That text hangs around the neck of millions of parents in our land—along with the millstone.

Parents and grandparents can do nothing better for their children than to share with them a personal faith in Christ. Our children do not need a bit of religion or a touch of morality, they need Christ; and parents are guilty of the worst of crimes if their children do not see faith in their parents. Children cannot trade on the faith of their parents, but they must see it so clearly that they will long to have their own.

Lois and Eunice were women of sincere faith

Paul referred to Timothy's faith as 'sincere', but immediately he adds that it was first found in his mother and grandmother (2 Timothy 1:5). He used a word with a small negative prefix, and what he actually said was that their faith was *unhypocritical*, though naturally the word had come to take on the positive meaning of something that is sincere or genuine.

In his first letter to Timothy, Paul had reminded the young pastor of the command that he had given Timothy when he first went down to Ephesus; in summary, concluded Paul, 'The goal of this command is love, which comes from a pure heart and a good conscience and a *sincere faith*' (1 Timothy 1:5). That is the exact description of the faith of Timothy's mother and grandmother. Notice how Paul described this faith: it was a sincere faith that 'first *lived* in your grandmother … and mother … and, I am persuaded, now *lives* in you also'. That is a powerful expression: a faith that lives! Living faith is a faith that has taken up residence; it is not passing and transitory, but is permanently at home and motivates the whole life.

But how do we see a 'sincere' living faith? James, in his New Testament letter, provided the answer to this when he was writing about the relationship between the privilege of justification by faith and the importance of good works. Some have concluded that James is at variance with Paul by suggesting that salvation is by works rather than through faith alone. But are these two contradictory? Not at all. When James wrote: 'You see that a person is justified by what he does and not by faith alone' (James 2:24), he expected us to place the emphasis in the correct place. Punctuation is very important in bringing out meaning. Place a comma after the word 'justified' and you will notice that a little comma makes a lot of difference. Thus we can read it: You can *see* that a person is justified [by faith]. How can you see that a person is justified by faith when we all know that you cannot see faith? The answer is that you can see a person's faith by what they do; and that will reveal the truth of their faith—whether or not they are hypocrites.

In other words, the Christian faith of these two women was revealed in their consistent lives; and that would not have been easy in a home where the father was perhaps frequenting the pagan temple of Zeus. But it also revealed the priority of Lois and Eunice for the life of Timothy: it was not his education, finding the right wife, getting the best career, making a fortune or maintaining good health—but coming to faith in Christ.

Holy Trinity Church is a small but attractive building in the pretty village of Bosham in Sussex. It is said to be the church where King Harold worshipped before he left for his fateful battle against the Norman invaders near Hastings in 1066, and supposedly where King Canute's second daughter was buried half a century earlier; but also, inside that place of worship is a marble plaque that reads:

Sacred to the memory of Lady Charlotte Berkeley, daughter of Charles, fourth Duke of Richmond, the affectionate and beloved wife of the Honourable Maurice Frederick Fitzharding-Berkely, Captain of the Royal Navy later became Admiral [enough of the men and now back to Lady Charlotte] Strong in faith, fervent in hope, a bright example of true Christian piety and moral fortitude. Her last and earnest prayer [was] that her children should be brought up in the fear and love of God. Died 19 August 1833 aged 28 years.

What a magnificent testimony. I would love to know the later story of her children, but I am sure that we will meet up with Charlotte in heaven, along with Lois and Eunice—God's little women.

Lois and Eunice were women of courageous faith

Eunice, a Jewess, was married to a non-Jew. We do not know how or why that came about, but even before her conversion to Christ that placed her in a very difficult position. Strict Jewish law did not recognize the marriage of a Jew and a pagan, and any children from such a union would be considered illegitimate. Eunice carried that stigma in the eyes of many Jews.

Deuteronomy 7:3–4 was taken seriously among the Jews; it was a warning against marriages with the surrounding pagan nations: 'Do not intermarry with them. Do not give your daughters to their sons or take their daughters for your sons, for they will turn your sons away from following me to serve other gods, and the Lord's anger will burn against you and will quickly destroy you.' There is wisdom there, because God knew that the nations would draw Israel away from true worship and pure morality—and that is precisely what did happen over the following centuries. It is still relatively easy for the unbelieving partner to drag the believing partner down and out of faith. There were doubtless tough times for Eunice, and she would never recommend what Paul elsewhere warns against: 'Do not be yoked together with unbelievers' (2 Corinthians 6:14). Not one Christian wife or husband with an unbelieving partner would recommend this arrangement.

However, by the time Paul was writing his letter to Timothy, Eunice had professed to follow Jesus of Nazareth. She was now doubly unfit to be considered among her own race. Many Jews were bitterly opposed to Paul's teaching, and they stoned him and left him for dead. The pagans were not too bothered by what they saw as a squabble among the Jews, and Eunice would find little sympathy from her husband who, if he held an important post, would be involved in the temple of Zeus. Perhaps Eunice tried every way to persuade him to come and hear Paul.

This will be familiar territory to some. But Eunice did not cave in and give up her faith. She obviously had a vision of what God could do for her boy. In her case, she was blessed with the valuable support of her own mother. Eunice named her boy 'I honour God', which is the meaning of 'Timothy'. It was a Greek name and perhaps it suited her husband who interpreted 'God' in another way.

Lystra, as we have already noted, was an extremely superstitious town.

Jupiter and Zeus were worshipped there, and there was a large temple just outside the city walls. Religion was everywhere—but it was the wrong religion. How Eunice must have valued her relationship with the new and true Israel of faith. We can imagine Timothy returning home after the stoning of Paul (2 Timothy 3:11) and enquiring of his mother: 'Does it have to be like this when you become a Christian?' and he would have received a clear answer in the affirmative.

This was an important lesson for Timothy, because he later suffered from poor health (Paul referred in 1 Timothy 5:23 to his 'frequent illnesses'), was timid by nature (1 Corinthians 16:10: 'If Timothy comes, see to it that he has nothing to fear while he is with you'), was looked down on by his opponents as an inexperienced young man (1 Timothy 4:12 and 2 Timothy 2:22 literally: 'Don't let anyone *think* down on you'), faced vigorous opposition from those with false doctrine, especially Hymenaeus and Alexander (1 Timothy 1:3–4, 19–20), and state persecution was never far away. It would appear that this young pastor at Ephesus was discouraged and perhaps even wavering, and in order to keep him on track, Paul could hardly do better than to twice remind him of the firm, unyielding faith of the two women who had most influenced his life: Eunice and Lois.

2 Timothy 1:5–7 is clearly a rallying cry to a demoralized soldier:

I have been reminded of your sincere faith, which first lived in your grandmother Lois and in your mother Eunice and, I am persuaded, now lives in you also. For this reason I remind you to fan into flame the gift of God, which is in you through the laying on of my hands. For God did not give us a spirit of timidity, but a spirit of power, of love and of self-discipline.

'For this reason' points back to the faith of Eunice and Lois. We need a generation of young people who are inspired to courageous faith by the example of their mother—or grandmother.

Bramwell, one of the sons of William and Katherine Booth, the founders of the Salvation Army, comments that as children they were once afraid that they would be laughed at in school as poor, because of the patches on their clothes. He recorded how their mother sat the children down and patiently explained that they were poor—and why. Bramwell concluded that by the time she had finished her lesson: 'Mother not only patched our clothes, but made us proud of the patches.' That was an example of a mother's courageous faith.

Paul returned to the same example in 2 Timothy 3:14 when he reminded Timothy about how convinced he was in his faith: 'Because you know those from whom you learned it.' These two women little realized how impressed Paul was with their resolute faith, and how easily he could use its example, years later, as a spur to this wounded soldier. Children and grandchildren are watching our faith, and that is an enormous privilege and challenge to God's little people. We should never underestimate their significance.

Lois and Eunice were women of contagious faith

They clearly had a passionate desire to ensure that their Timothy would learn about their faith—and learn it from the beginning. John Calvin, the French Reformer of the sixteenth century, commented on Timothy that 'He had been educated in such a manner that he might have sucked godliness along with his milk.' The reason why Eunice is mentioned in Acts 16:11 is because clearly she was already well known as a Christian. Even before her conversion she must have had an enthusiastic hope for the coming of the Jewish Messiah, and when Paul preached about Jesus of Nazareth it took little to persuade her that this was the one she was looking for. From then on, everyone among the Jewish community in Lystra knew that Eunice was a follower of the 'the Way'. She believed that if a faith is worth having, it is worth sharing.

It is the odd view of some that we must not influence our children—they must be left to make up their own minds. But we do not hold the same attitude to eating, sleeping or education—or even their firsts friends. Some things are too important to be left to choice. In reality, every parent influences their children in a thousand ways from sport to hobbies, and from politics to religion. If we leave the matter of relationship to God for our children to decide on later, we have already influenced them—we have told them that the subject is not worth significant attention.

Evangelism begins in the home. Every parent shares their faith with their children: faith in self, in the family name, in society, in education, in nothing or in God. Some years ago a young man in New York committed suicide and left a note which said: 'My parents taught me to believe in God—and that he did not matter.'

No parents should leave the spiritual education of their children to others. The contagion of our own enthusiasm for God should permeate the whole of family life. No doubt Eunice and Lois were convinced of the truthfulness of the Hebrew Scriptures, and they taught Timothy what Paul later had only to remind him of, that they were 'God breathed' (2 Timothy 3:16). As a child, Timothy learnt that the stories were true and the doctrine was true. Without this conviction, mother and grandmother had no authority. Parents without a trusted Bible, just as a church without a trusted Bible, are like a crocodile without teeth: they can open their mouth as wide as they like—but who cares?

Children are always asking questions 'Why?' and 'Why not?' They must have biblical answers that come from parents who enthusiastically and courageously live out the word of God in front of their children.

Lois and Eunice were women of patient faith

In his book *God's Good Life*, which is a commentary on the Ten Commandments, David Field offers a telling story related by an Archbishop in the House of Lords. It was a piece of extended writing by an eight-year-old boy on 'What a grandmother is'. Part of it went like this:

A grandmother is a lady who has no children of her own, so she likes other people's little girls and boys. A grandfather is a man grandmother. He goes for walks with the boys and they talk about fishing and tractors. Grandmothers don't have to do anything but be there. They are old, so they shouldn't have to play hard or run. They should never say, 'Hurry up' … They don't have to be smart, only answer questions like why dogs hate cats and why God isn't married. They don't talk baby-talk like visitors. When they read to us, they don't skip bits, or mind if it is the same story over again. Everybody should have one, especially if you don't have television, because grandmothers are the only grown-ups who have time.

There seems little doubt that Lois and Eunice had time for Timothy. We don't know whether he was the only child in the home or whether there was a whole houseful of children, but what we do know is that the two women in his young life had patient time for him. They clearly invested 'quality time' in quality training. But what is so interesting is that in spite of all their careful instruction, they did not lead Timothy to Christ—Paul did.

Timothy did not come to personal faith in Christ as a child; how could he, when at Lystra so little would have been known of Jesus of Nazareth until Paul and Barnabas arrived in AD 47? But the patient foundation had been laid. Carefully they had steered his mind away from Zeus, and their prayers doubtless continued as he grew into his teenage years. No doubt it would have been instructive to have heard them at prayer for Timothy in the midst of a pagan culture. But Timothy was in his teens before he yielded to Christ under the ministry of Paul.

Preparing the soil and sowing the seed can be a laborious business. We bring children and grandchildren to church, teach and train them, pray and worry over them. But for years there is no result. That is not the time to give up in despair. Patience is demanded. Eunice and Lois sowed the seed, Paul watered, but it was God who brought the harvest. When the American evangelist, Dwight L Moody was preaching in the Metropolitan Tabernacle in London on the occasion of the Jubilee of Charles Haddon Spurgeon in 1884, he commented, 'His mother I have not met, but most good men have praying mothers, God bless them.' That was certainly true of Timothy, except that he had the double blessing of a praying grandmother also.

Lois and Eunice were women of biblical faith

What led Lois and Eunice to faith? It may have been ultimately the preaching of Paul, but originally it was the reading of the Hebrew Scriptures—our Old Testament. When Luke commented in Acts 16:2 that 'The brothers at Lystra and Iconium spoke well of [Timothy]', it was clear that he had a reputation for godliness, clear biblical thinking and reliability. From whom did he learn all that? From his mother and grandmother. And where did they learn this? From all that Paul listed in 2 Timothy 3:16, it is clear that Lois and Eunice were constantly applying the Scriptures to life in front of Timothy: they knew that the Scriptures were 'useful for teaching, rebuking, correcting and training in righteousness'.

Doubtless Lois and Eunice were well aware of the proverb: 'Train a child in the way he should go, and when he is old he will not turn from it' (Proverbs 22:6), and they applied this wisely to their upbringing of Timothy. They would have taught him the Hebrew Scriptures and, if he had attended a Jewish school, the faith of Judaism would have been reinforced there. Clearly they prepared the mind of Timothy for the coming of the Messiah. And all this, according to Paul, 'from infancy' (2 Timothy 3:15).

The word Paul used is *brephos,* and it has to mean a young child. It is used of the child in the womb and the new-born infant as well as the young child. There is no word in either Hebrew (the language of the Old Testament) or Greek (the language of the New Testament) for an embryo; that word is an invention of our modern world because then it can destroy a child with a clear conscience; but it is a word that the Christian should never use with reference to the human race. The biblical word for that which is in the womb from the moment of conception is a child. The Hebrew is *yeleth* and the Greek is *brephos.* Paul is referring to a small child. There is another word Paul could have used if he meant an older child.

Timothy was taught the Hebrew Scriptures long before Eunice and Lois knew the Messiah for themselves; but they were expecting the Messiah and taught young Timothy to expect him also.

Christian parents should have an equally firm expectation of the second coming of Christ.

Perhaps Eunice and Lois taught him Jewish stories as well. There is nothing wrong with good stories—every child loves a story—but we must not neglect the best story of all. It is the Bible alone that can make our children 'wise for salvation' (2 Timothy 3:15). Many books can provide enjoyment, others can offer knowledge and a few can impart wisdom, but only one can make our children perfectly 'wise for salvation'.

Sadly, the 'family altar' has become an old-fashioned concept in the frenetic rush of our modern Christian homes; that is a tragedy, and we are reaping a bitter harvest as more and more children from Christian families are sliding into the world and abandoning the faith of their parents. There can be little doubt that Lois and Eunice prayed over Timothy before he was born, and added reading the Scriptures immediately afterwards. Many Christian parents whose children have long since flown the nest, bitterly regret not having had regular family prayers; and many teenagers from Christian homes cannot remember praying with their parents after the age of five or six.

These two little women left a legacy for which the church over the past two thousand years must be grateful. Timothy ministered at Ephesus: he was sickly, timid and facing mountainous opposition, but what if he had had a different mother? No doubt that, if she lived into old age, Eunice was still praying for him all through his ministry. Christian mothers and grandmothers have an enormous influence over their young children. They are God's little women. Thank God for them.

Phoebe—sister, servant, saint

'I commend to you our sister Phoebe, a servant of the church in Cenchrea. I ask you to receive her in the Lord in a way worthy of the saints and to give her any help she may need from you, for she has been a great help to many people, including me' Romans 16:1–2

The final chapter of Romans is one of the most interesting parts of the whole of Paul's letter to the church in Rome. It is what brings his message alive with human reality, and it stops us from thinking that this is a book of theoretical Christian theology to the church in general but to no one in particular. Paul concludes with a list of people to whom he sends greetings; the people who will hear this letter read and would be encouraged to act upon it.

Some commentators believe that this list of names in Romans 16 does not really belong to the church at Rome at all, but was originally part of another letter to Ephesus which somehow became detached and needs to be put back there; they tell us that unfortunately we do not have that particular letter to the Ephesians and this is all that remains! It is suggested that 15:33 would be a nice place to end the letter: 'the God of peace be with you all. Amen.' On the other hand we might as easily claim that 11:33–36 would also be a good place to end the letter: 'For from him and through him and to him are all things. To him be the glory for ever! Amen.' But in reality these are not where Paul decided to end his letter, and we should allow him to decide where he concludes. One reason for such theories is that Paul had never been to Rome, so he could not possibly know so many Christians there—which overlooks the frequent interaction between the churches and Paul's deep and affectionate relationship with the members. Sufficient to say that there is no copy of the letter to the Romans ever circulating without chapter 16 to close it, and since these are academic theories without substantial foundation, we do not need to spend any more time on them.

Some of the people here in the church at Rome had already been with Paul elsewhere, and they were commonly known. Priscilla and Aquila are an example (v 3). According to 1 Corinthians 16:19, shortly before Paul wrote this letter to the Romans, they were in Ephesus, but Priscilla and Aquila spent half their life moving from place to place; they moved at least four or five times within the space of the New Testament.

However, it is this woman Phoebe who attracts our interest. In a student meeting, a girl asked me what I thought about Paul's attitude to women. She admitted she did not know her Bible well, but didn't he have a rather negative and low regard for women? In reply I suggested that she should read Ephesians 5:25 as a good starting point: 'Husbands, love your wives, as Christ loved the church and gave himself up for her'; I put it to her that any woman who is loved by her husband like that, may well consider herself to be happy indeed. I could have turned her to Phoebe here in Romans 16, but it would have taken me a little longer to explain, and I didn't have time.

There are no fewer than eight women listed by Paul in this chapter. Phoebe was almost certainly the one who took the letter from Corinth to Rome, since the royal mail was reserved only for government correspondence. All else had to be transported by merchants or trusted friends; there was simply no other way of moving personal letters across the Empire, and therefore if Phoebe was on her way to Rome in the course of her business, it was appropriate that the apostle would have taken advantage of her travel for this reliable service. Paul would only entrust his letters to people of integrity, since already some were beginning to write letters pretending to be from the apostle; this is why, on a number of occasions, he signed off a letter by drawing attention to his own personal signature (1 Corinthians 16:21; Galatians 6:11; Colossians 4:18; 2 Thessalonians 3:17; Philemon 19).

God chose a woman to carry his Son into the world via Bethlehem, and he chose a woman to carry into the world via Rome the greatest letter of Christian theology ever written.

Almost certainly Phoebe was a wealthy business woman. She may well have been a widow or otherwise unmarried, because it would have been unusual for her to be travelling on her own if she was married; and she almost certainly had business interests in the Roman world. The word that is used of the help the church should offer her—and which reflects her assistance to the church at Cenchrea—is *pragmati* (v 2), from which we get our word 'pragmatic' meaning 'concerned with practical matters'. In the first century it was commonly used to refer to legal affairs; it is used in this context in 1 Corinthians 6:1 of Christians taking each other to court. However, we cannot conclude from this that Phoebe was working in the law, though she may have been. Like Lydia, she was clearly a business woman, since the word can refer to anything from a legal action to a trouble or difficulty via business or trade. The *New King James Version* has 'in whatever business she has need of you'. That is a clumsy way of expressing it, but it is fairly accurate.

The postscript on Phoebe in this letter from Paul was in fact a letter of commendation, which reminds us of the regular correspondence that went on between the churches and the many visits that were made. Such letters and visits held the churches together in fellowship and prayer, and guarded against false teaching and rumour. The constant interaction between the churches with letters and couriers was vital to the health of the infant church. And always the letters were entrusted to reliable people. Tychicus was one such, who carried a vital letter on his way down to Colosse and delivered a very personal note from Paul to Philemon. Letters of commendation were familiar in the first century. If wealthy citizens had a son or daughter travelling across the empire, they would carry with them a letter to ensure that they could find secure hospitality in a villa or mansion each night. Churches still use letters of commendation today so that when a Christian moves from one area to another, their 'home' church can vouch for their good standing in Christ. In the case of Phoebe it was also a guarantee that the letter she carried from Paul was authentic.

Without a doubt Phoebe was well thought of in the church at Cenchrea which was a small town but a very important one. It was the eastern port of Corinth, a large and cosmopolitan city in Greece. Cenchrea was about seven miles from the city and was a vital trade route and the centre of commerce with the whole of the eastern Mediterranean coast all the way up to Italy itself. The town had expanded significantly in recent years and now boasted a harbour that was about eight hectares in area—some twenty acres. The waterfront where the ships tied up to offload their cargo was well over half a mile long (one kilometre). Paul had preached the gospel here, and he used this port when he first left Corinth (Acts 18:18). If Phoebe was converted at this time—and it is very likely she was, because as far as we know that was the first time that Cenchrea heard the gospel—then she could not have been a Christian more than six or seven years. But already she was well known in the church and in good standing.

Evidently Phoebe was born into a pagan family, since no Jewish or Christian parents would have given their daughter the name of the moon goddess in Greek mythology—Phoebus; she was the sister of Apollo and Diana. As a matter of interest, in this list in Romans 16 there are at least three other Christians who carried names associated with the Greek gods: in verse 14 there is a man called Hermes and in verse 15 one called Nereus (the old man of the sea), and in the same verse we read of Olympas. That reveals the background of many of these young Christians, and yet they saw no need to change their names when they became Christians; they learnt from the apostle Paul that the gods of this world are nothing, so that it was a matter of indifference whether they changed their name or not. Besides, Phoebe's name meant radiant, and that was an appropriate name for someone who had been brought out of the darkness of paganism into the light of the gospel of Jesus Christ. Phoebe was doubtless a radiant Christian.

Phoebe the sister

Some in the church at Rome were actually members of Caesar's household staff (Philippians 4:22), and others held high positions in the civil service at a time when the Emperor was increasingly showing signs of the cruelty and megalomania for which he would shortly be condemned by the Senate. To all of these, whether slaves or free, high or low in society, Phoebe was, without distinction, a sister in Christ. Phoebe would be reminded that on one occasion Jesus had turned to the crowds and declared: 'Whoever does the will of my Father in heaven is my brother and sister and mother' (Matthew 12:50).

Dozens of times in his letters Paul refers to his readers as 'brothers'. That was a generic term to cover both men and women; it was a label of new birth, referring to those who were born by the Holy Spirit into a new family.

Jesus is 'the firstborn among many brothers' (Romans 8:29). According to the letter to the Hebrews: 'Both the one who makes men holy and those who are made holy are of the same family. So Jesus is not ashamed to call them brothers' (Hebrews 2:11). Jesus, in all his perfect pure holiness is not ashamed to call Phoebe and all the Christians in Rome, his sisters and brothers. What magnificent grace!

But why, particularly, did Paul refer to Phoebe as a 'sister'? It was not a common description that he used; in fact the only other occasions when he used the designation with reference to a particular individual are in v 15 'Nereus and his sister', and Philemon 2, 'Apphia our sister'. Perhaps Paul wished to remind the Christians at Rome that although they had never met Phoebe, and she came to them as a complete stranger, she was, nevertheless, part of the universal family of Christians. The 'family of believers', which is so beautifully and accurately translated in Galatians 6:10, is one of the special privileges of the Christian faith. But unlike some religions, it is not a family in defence of which we are expected to carry out fanatical attacks and kill and maim innocent people, rather it is a family to whom 'as we have opportunity … we do good'. According to Paul, whilst Christians should do good to everybody, quite unashamedly, members of the family must take precedence.

But there is more in this relationship than simply helping one another. Many families in the first century, as in the twenty-first, were tragically dysfunctional. Divorce was as commonplace then as now, with all its sad consequences for partners and children. Others in the time of Paul were thrown out of their homes when they professed Christ—and this also is the experience of many living under the rule of intolerant religions today. In addition, slaves had no family that they could call their own; even the male who married—though only with the permission of his master—did not own his wife or his children and could be sold separately from them.

The Christian family, however, is a new and permanent relationship in which the members of the family cannot walk out on each other. Whether we like it or not, we are brothers and sisters. We will not always be the best of friends, since we can choose our friends but we do not choose our relatives; however, they are chosen for us by God. It was this family relationship that would mean so much to the early Christians. The idea of this total stranger being a 'sister' to the family in Rome was as exciting as it was novel to the Christians there.

What was even more revolutionary in first-century Rome was the fact that this new relationship cut across all social divides. The class structure across the empire was both rigid and jealously guarded, no less than in eighteenth and nineteenth-century England. Everyone knew their place— and remained there. However, Phoebe's relationship as a sister in Christ had nothing to do with her status in society. Nowhere is this better illustrated than in the example of Onesimus. When Paul wrote his letter to Philemon, it was to accompany a runaway slave who belonged to the estate of Philemon. Onesimus had stolen, run away and ended up in Rome where he made contact with Paul and was converted. The apostle followed the usual custom of the day and sent Onesimus back to his master, but with this difference: he was being sent back 'No longer as a slave, but better than a slave, as a dear brother' (Philemon 16). He would still be in service and would now serve more loyally than ever before, but the relationship was one of brothers from now on. That was unbelievable in first-century Roman society.

Phoebe the servant

Paul also described Phoebe as a 'servant' of the church in Cenchrea. There has been some debate over this word. It is the feminine of the Greek noun *diakonos*, a common word in the first century that simply referred to a servant. Later in the life of the church it was more formally employed as a title of a group of leaders or workers whose qualifications Paul outlined in his letters to Timothy and Titus. For this reason, some have concluded that Phoebe was a 'deaconess' in this technical sense, and others have expanded this to defend women in spiritual leadership and even pastoral ministry and preaching. This is not what Paul meant to imply at all. At this time in the church there is no evidence of 'deaconesses' as an office or group of women in the church. All that Paul intended was that Phoebe served the church in any way that she could: humbly, gladly and willingly. To make more of it than this is to read far more than is justified into the text.

It is likely that Phoebe was a well-placed business woman—not at all uncommon in the first century as we saw with Lydia—and one who regularly travelled from Greece to Italy in the course of her trade, and yet she was a servant of the churches. According to Paul, she had been a great help to many people, including himself—though exactly how, we are not told. We would love to know in what way she had been a help, but what we do know is that she served the church at Cenchrea in whatever way she could.

But Paul used another word to describe the servant ministry of Phoebe. When he referred to her as 'a great help to many people', he employed a word that may have a double meaning. The word *prostatis* was used in the Greek and Roman world of a guardian of the gods, and that was not a job only for men, but also for women. Not all women were tied to the home as a virtual slave of their husband. On the contrary there were very wealthy women who we read about in secular writings, and some of them, because of their wealth, became guardians of the pagan temples. In the story of Mary Magdalene we referred to Eumachia at Pompeii and Theodora at Corinth who held just such a position. These women were expected to use their personal resources for the support of the temple of the gods; this was considered a great privilege, and the word that was used for this was *prostatis*, the word that Paul used here.

Paul was quite unashamed in taking over a word that was often used in the first century to describe priestesses looking after the temple with their personal resources, and applying it to a Christian doing the same for the people of God. Perhaps the double meaning here is that it is possible this was exactly what Phoebe had been involved in before her conversion. Conceivably she had once applied her wealth to the support of a pagan temple, but now everything had changed. Phoebe shared with God's people in need just as Lydia had done. She too was a busineswoman who gave her resources—in her case her home as well as her wealth—for the church and the apostles. There are many women throughout the Gospels and in the letters of Paul who are described as having a ministry of caring. The mother of Rufus was singled out by Paul as having been like a mother to him also (v 13). Earlier, Paul had used a form of this same word to refer to those with gifts of 'leadership' in the church (Romans 12:8), and he would use it again in his letter to Timothy (1 Timothy 5:17 'Elders that rule'), but the emphasis is always the same: giving ourselves and our means for the service of the people of God.

Phoebe was neither selfish nor selective, and therefore when she came to Rome, Paul wanted the church there to treat her just as she has been caring for the church in Cenchrea. How well would the Christians care for us if it was in the same measure that we had cared for them? Our Lord set the principle that 'With the measure you use, it will be measured to you' (Mark 4:24). It must have been such a joy for Phoebe to arrive in the large metropolis of Rome where perhaps she knew only her worldly business contacts, and to find herself immediately accepted into a loving and caring family. She had no need to put up in the local hostelry because the homes of Christian brothers and sisters were open to her. Hospitality, according to Paul, is one of the gifts of the Spirit (Romans 12:13) and if the church had not already opened its homes to Phoebe, it would after this letter was read!

Phoebe the saint

Why did Paul refer to Phoebe as a saint? The word means holy; but he was not referring to the fact that she belonged to a religious order, nor did he mean that her great service or her giving made her a saint. It was a word that Paul commonly used, and early in this letter he addressed, 'All in Rome who are loved by God and called [to be] saints'. Almost forty times in his letters the apostle referred to Christians under this title; see for example Romans 15:25,26,31; 16:15 where it is very clear that Paul is referring to the whole church and not to an elite band of super-saints within it. Whilst most translations agree with the NIV by inserting the words 'to be' in this phrase in Romans 1:7, the verb is not there in the Greek and it would be better to read: 'called saints'. It is their name rather than their objective that is in view here.

Whilst it is true that all Christians are expected to be holy, what is even more significant is that in Christ they have been *declared* holy. Or, as he explained to the Corinthians: 'You were washed, you were sanctified, you were justified in the name of the Lord Jesus Christ and by the Spirit of our God' (1 Corinthians 6:11); here, the word 'sanctified' is the same root word as the word 'saints'. When the righteousness of Christ is reckoned to the account of a man or woman, they are declared and seen to be holy in the sight of God, and on this basis alone they can be 'justified' or declared not guilty.

Sadly, the Roman Catholic denomination has taken the word out of its Bible context and has given it an entirely different meaning, so we have Saint Francis and Saint Alban and thousands more. Past leaders of Roman Catholicism are 'canonized' (declared saints) after their death providing some miracle can be associated with them. These people—which includes Thomas More who, as Chancellor to Henry VIII, burnt alive more evangelical Christians than his predecessors or successors—apparently lived such holy lives that we can share in their works of 'supererogation', which means works above what they needed to do. All this has ruined a beautiful word that, in the New Testament, exclusively refers to all who have been justified by faith in the cross and resurrection of Christ alone.

For a moment we will imagine Phoebe giving her testimony to the church in Rome. There is, of course, a degree of supposition here because we know little about her background, but there is no reason why all of it may not be true:

I was brought up in a pagan family. My father was a wealthy government official and merchant, and when my parents died I inherited the estate of my father as the only daughter. It put me in possession of a good income and I was expected to follow the example of my father and support the work at the local temple—which I did gladly. As a result, I was highly respected in the town. I had been named after the moon goddess, and I was delighted with this and counted it a privilege. I lived in a seaport, and like most seaports everything revolved around making money and pleasure. There was nothing in the Roman mythology of gods and goddesses that would restrain our life of self-gratification and greed. The deities never laid restraints upon us, and they had no moral standards to set us; they didn't care and they were generally amoral at best or immoral at worst.

Then one day Paul came preaching. I can see him now as he stood on the waterfront. Many of the sailors mocked and jeered, and some jostled him, but he carried on preaching. A few of us gathered around, particularly the women, because there was something about what he said that rang a chord in our own heart and life. He talked about the Son of God, Jesus of Nazareth, who the Romans had crucified in Jerusalem some years back. He told us the real meaning of his death was that this Jesus of Nazareth was the one promised in the Hebrew Scriptures long before, from the time of the beginning of the world on through a man called Moses and through the whole of their Scriptures. Then Paul went on to say that when he did come, he lived a perfect and sinless life and he died on the cross, was buried in a tomb, and—fantastically—he rose again from the dead and was seen by all his followers. Then he returned to heaven from where one day he will come again at the end of the world.

But Paul didn't leave it there, because so far we could scoff and say, 'Well, we're not going to fall into the trap of believing that sort of rubbish.' Paul began to tell us what it all meant. He told us that the reason why Jesus died on the cross was to take upon himself all our guilt and our sin and the foulness of everything we had done against a holy God. It was as if he had done it all in place of us, so that I, Phoebe, could be forgiven by a holy God. More than that, Paul said that I would know that God had taken my unrighteousness and put it to Christ's account and had taken Christ's righteousness and put it to my account. So that when God sees me he sees me not with my sin but with the sinlessness of Jesus Christ. I could be free from my guilt, my sin and my punishment; my conscience could be clean, and I could know freedom and peace with God and a friendship with the one true and only God.

It all made sense. I didn't know at the time, but it was the Holy Spirit working in my mind and my heart to make it make sense to me. That's how I became a Christian. My life was changed, I was converted. From now on I knew that I was holy, not because I did nothing wrong—because I do—but because God sees me as holy as his Son, Jesus. That is why I am a saint. And that is why all my brothers and sisters in the church at Cenchreae and Corinth, and here in Rome and all across the empire where churches have been established, are called 'saints'. Of course we are to live holy lives as well, but the great thing is that the past has been rubbed out and we have had a new start because we have been declared clean by God.

They were mixed congregations at Corinth and Cenchrea and Rome. These cities were cosmopolitan centres where people from all nations were coming in and out all the time; quite a few languages were spoken, though fortunately everyone spoke the common language of Greek because that was the way you got on in business. The young Christian congregations were similarly a mixture: some were converted Jews and others, like Phoebe herself, were converted Gentiles and pagans; some were slaves, freedmen, slave owners and Roman citizens, rich, poor, educated and uneducated. But to them all, Phoebe was a sister, a servant and a saint. That was her privilege and her responsibility.

Index

Index

Index

ALSO BY BRIAN EDWARDS

GOD'S LITTLE PEOPLE
—IN PAUL'S LETTERS

BRIAN H EDWARDS

For every person whose name blazes across the pages of our heritage of history in the large letters of a Tyndale, Bunyan, Wesley, Spurgeon or Lloyd-Jones, there are tens of thousands of 'little people' who have courageously and faithfully maintained a stand for the truth and have extended the borders of the Kingdom of God. It is upon these that the Lord builds his church and they are equally important in God's large strategy for the gospel. Most of us are precisely that—just little people. Here is the story of some of those little people whom Paul takes great delight in introducing into his letters. This is a book to encourage every Christian faithfully at work in the church today.

112PP, PAPERBACK, £5
ISBN 1 903087 85 6

GOD'S LITTLE PEOPLE
—THE APOSTLES OF JESUS

BRIAN H EDWARDS

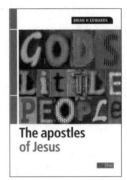

For all their importance, most of the apostles of Jesus have very little on record either of what they said or what they did. For some, we do not have a single word that they spoke, and others appear only as a name in a list. Apart from Peter and John, they all pass from our view as individuals after the first chapter of Acts; James only reappears in time to be executed by Herod. Like all of us, these 'little people' worshipped, worked and went. But then the whole purpose of our lives, as theirs, is not that we should leave a name for ourselves but that we should exalt the name of Christ. John the Baptist set the compass bearing for the journey of the apostles of Christ—and for all who follow them: 'He must become greater; I must become less' (John 3:30). Few have exhibited this so well as the twelve apostles.

128PP, PAPERBACK, £5
ISBN 1 903087 94 5, REF: GLP 2

DA VINCI
A BROKEN CODE

BRIAN H EDWARDS

Is *The Da Vinci Code* just a harmless novel, or is there something more dangerous or even dishonest about it? If the New Testament Gospels are in its sights, what is it that is causing such a stir? And how should a reader respond to it? Is it to be ignored or taken head on? Is it a powerful tool, or is it just another broken hammer? Are its claims true or...

£10 for five copies—

Discounts for quantity orders.
Please enquire for details

32PP BOOKLET, £2.50
ISBN 1 84625 019 6

THE DIVINE SUBSTITUTE

THE ATONEMENT IN THE BIBLE
AND HISTORY

BRIAN H EDWARDS
IAN SHAW

The purpose of this book is to demonstrate that the doctrine of propitiatory atonement is the principal way—though not the only way—in which the Bible views the death of Christ, and that this has been consistently taught at every period of the story of the church.

128PP £6
ISBN 1 84625 038 2